The Assassination of Heydrich

Hitler's Hangman and the Czech Resistance

©2012 Zuzana Wiener

All rights reserved. Printed in the United States of America. No part of this book may be used or reproduced in any manner without written permission except for brief quotations for review purposes only.

Irie Books
12699 Cristi Way
Bokeelia, Florida 33922

ISBN 10: 1-61720-372-6
ISBN 13: 978-1-51543-903-5
First Edition

10 9 8 7 6 5 4 3 2 1

Originally published by Grossman Publishers, Inc. 1969

Cover design: ital art by Mariah Fox
www.mariahfox.com

Acknowledgment:
Heydrichiada by Cestmar Amort, Nase Vojsko, Prague
Stopa Ved K Renemu, Rudolf Strobinger, Lidova Demokracie, Prague
Bomba Pro Heydricha, Dusan Hamsik & Jiri Prazak, Mlada Fronta, Prague
Not Only Black Uniforms, Miroslav Ivanov, Nase Vojsko, Prague

The Assassination of Heydrich

Hitler's Hangman and the Czech Resistance

Jan Wiener

CONTENTS

Foreword–7
Invaders–9
Occupation–13
Escape–21
Resistance–24
Game of Chess–32
Heydrich's Assignment–39
Rails to Freedom–49
Franta and Moravek–53
In Prison–64
Paratroopers' Assignment–67
Catholic Jew–79
Hunt and Reprisals–82
On the Rock–100
Final Resistance–102
On the Run–135
Yalta and the Liberation–141
Photos–143
Author Biography–161
Author Chronology–162
Honors–166
Memory of Jan Wiener–168

Foreword

The name Reinhard Heydrich may not mean much to contemporary readers in this country. It is true that there are a number of people who remember his name and the fact that he was assassinated during World War II. Some people remember Lidice and the shock that was felt in the world when this village was totally destroyed in reprisal for Heydrich's death. But few people will know the atmosphere that prevailed in occupied Czechoslovakia, the fear and terror, during the period called the Heydrichiade.

This, then, is the story of the assassination of Reinhard Heydrich by the Czech people. It has been pieced together years afterward from survivors' and peripheral participants' recollections, from various documents, and from Nazi records. I was only a peripheral participant, as I was forced to leave Prague after the occupation, but my story—aside from being fairly typical of the Czech refugee—touches the lives of some of the main characters in the resistance. I have included it as a frame of reference which the reader can perhaps identify with. It will also help to explain my knowledge of various activities and strategies employed by the resistance.

The issues at stake in this book are especially alive for the Czechs and Slovaks. Through a period of more than six hundred years the Czechs learned how to live as an oppressed minority and how to survive. In 1918 they were largely responsible for the breakup of the Austro-Hungarian Empire with its unjust minority polity.

In a small occupied country in which the population is defenseless and exposed to the harsh measures of the occupier, the desire to survive is enormous as is the fear of violent death. Some people when faced with decisions that involve their own safety become so overwhelmed by the will to survive and the fear of death that they do things which under normal conditions they would not do. Others are able to master their fears and to help and to fight back.

To these people I dedicate this book. Some of them for one night sheltered people who were marked by the Gestapo. Some gave food. Others knew but did not inform. Others, again, were active saboteurs and national avengers.

Jan Wiener
Lenox, Massachusetts
June 1969

The Invaders

Both of my parents were born in Bohemia, which became part of Czechoslovakia when it was created in 1918. They grew up, met, and married in Prague. After World War I they moved to Hamburg where, in 1920, I was born. I lived among German people, went to school in Germany, and naturally learned to speak fluent German.

After Hitler came to power in 1933, pressures against Jews forced those of us who could manage to leave Germany to do so. We Wieners moved back to my parents' native country, where my grandmother still lived. I went to school in Prague, learned the Czech language, and learned to love the country and the people who had given us—and many other refugees— asylum and a new home.

Czechoslovakia at that time was a country with a very liberal democratic political system, therefore a country in which it was good to live. My friends were Czech boys. Through my friends I became actively involved in the cause of Czechoslovakia. By the time of the first general mobilization of the Czech army in 1938 when I was seventeen, I had so identified with this small nation that of course I volunteered to help fight for its integrity.

I was sent, as an infantry soldier, to the Giant Mountains in the northeast sector, bordering Germany.

We all expected to be fighting Germany at any moment, but we were confident that England and France, with whom Czechoslovakia had a pact of mutual military assistance, would come to our aid when we were attacked. However, in September of 1938, Sir Neville Chamberlain and Edouard Daladier formed the "Munich Agreement" with Mussolini and Hitler. Our borders, including the Sudetenland, were conceded by them to belong to Germany; Teschen was handed to the Poles; Czecho-Slovakia was hyphenated and declared two autonomous states. Besides crippling our transportation system, our economy, and shattering our national morale, this dismemberment made defense impossible as it took from us our fortified border mountains. The carving up of Czechoslovakia and the handing of our strategic territories to Hitler on a platter were supposed to appease his hunger. His demands were to end there; our sacrifice would bring "peace in our time."

It is still deeply imprinted on my memory how we Czechoslovak boys, so eager, so primed to fight for our national existence, were sent home from the border. The appeasement of Hitler's appetite for territory lasted five and a half months. He violated the Munich Pact—as he did all other agreements.

Shedding our uniforms reluctantly, the farm boys went back to their farms and others returned to jobs, while soldiers in the regular army had to sit around in barracks doing busywork. I returned to my schoolboy routine.

My father had left for Yugoslavia and my mother was anxious for me to follow him. I had my schoolboy's free ticket to the theater once a week, I had sports, I had friends, and I had the Sokol.

The Sokol (which means Falcons, or Hawks) then was a national physical-training society to which many belonged. There was a Sokol gymnasium in each community to which the men and boys on men's nights and the women and girls on women's nights went to exercise. Here we also cemented friendships; we met and admired leading gymnasts of other communities during frequent exchange visits and social affairs.

I know of no comparable institution in other countries which so completely erased class lines: here the banker, the farmer, the butcher all appeared in their gym suits to take part. Needless to say, there was no occupational guarantee that any of these would look more handsome than the others; in Sokol each man earned his fellows' esteem through personal ability. The Sokol was abolished by the Communist government in 1948. In 1956 it was, because of its popularity, reinstalled but under Communistic ideals.

I, my friends, my chemistry professor, and my mailman all spent many evenings each week at Sokol. It was here that political discussions would arise among the men; heads would be shaken, fists pounded. It was here that our natural leaders in any resistance would come to the fore.

It was snowing as I walked to school on that March 15 morning. When I arrived in class, our professor was not yet there. The radio was barking a harsh warning to us to stand by for important news; other students stood around in wondering attitudes. Then the teacher arrived. We turned to him for information and were stunned by his bleak expression; at the same moment the radio announced that the Germans were already in Bohemia and would reach Prague by eleven o'clock! Our national anthem was played—for the last time—while we stared at each other, not wholly believing. Then our teacher announced that he had orders to dismiss us; he advised us to go directly home.

We joined the shocked, silent people in the street. We drifted with them down to Wenceslas Square in the dense, heavy snow. The square quickly filled with a crowd which stood waiting in silence. Karel Bergmann, Vlasta Chervinka, and I stood together, waiting.

When the motorized infantry came, some people thrust their hands into their pockets and only glared, some made threatening gestures with their fists. Many women were crying.

But nobody shouted. Through the steady-falling snowflakes one could hear only the engines. The cold built up inside of us as well as outside as we watched the invaders roll by.

"England won't stand for this!" muttered Karel, hardly moving his lips. "War will be declared!"

Vlasta, white and trembling, nodded. "But if England doesn't fight—we must!" he said savagely. "We must!"

Both Karel and I turned to stare at him, surprised. He was a quiet studious boy, not one to be expected to wage war singlehanded. His words, brave though they were, made us even more deeply aware of our country's helplessness; our only real hope was the conscience of the world—and that conscience, we knew in our bones, had already slept peacefully through six years of Hitler's brutality.

But I agreed with Vlasta. I could not see quietly accepting Hitler's plans for us Czechs. We had heard, via the grapevine, that he was going to "Germanize" Bohemia. What would this mean? We were scared, depressed, and very angry. We wanted to fight—but with what? With snowballs? After a while we separated, each anxious to see how his own family would fare.

We exchanged the usual "See you tomorrow." But we did not know....

The Occupation

The historical background of this story goes back to before the Crown of St. Wenceslas. I have chosen to simplify since Czechoslovakia's entire history as an independent nation is contained within the memory of many adults.

After its formation in 1918, the Czechoslovak Republic enjoyed a healthy economic and political life for almost twenty years. Led by its enlightened first president, Thomas Masaryk, until he retired (at eighty-five) in 1935, it was able to weather the difficulties inherent in its makeup of several different national minorities better than its neighboring small states. Its highly developed industries, balanced by large agricultural areas, provided a good working ratio among peasants, middle classes, and industrial workers—an equalitarian atmosphere in which democracy and freedom could thrive. After 1933, however, Hitler's "Aryan supremacy" theories found a foothold among the, German-speaking Czech nationals along the northern border, in what Hitler called his "Sudetenland." Through Nazi-sponsored pressure and propaganda, many of these became persuaded that, as Germans, they were superior to Slavs, and that their fortunes were tied to Germany's. It was this hook on which Hitler hung his claim for annexing the Czech borderlands.

After the traitorous Munich agreement, which left "Czecho- Slovakia" without its natural mountainous borders and fortifications, the political leaders of the crippled and defenseless country did not share Chamberlain's euphoria. Hoping to form a government-in-exile to preserve Czechoslovakia's national entity and to protect its people from Hitler's insatiability, President Benes left Prague and went to London, there to join the Czech ambassador, Jan Masaryk, in his futile attempts to convince the British that war must be declared. In England, however, a shamed, sullen peace was being celebrated; the British government, committed to Munich, would not recognize the exile and therefore could not condone the government. Nevertheless, Czech patriots continued to leave the country; officers of the dismembered army, and others, joined Benes and Masaryk or went to Russia, Poland, or Yugoslavia to seek help and to organize resistance.

One of these was General Josef Bartik of the Czechoslovak Intelligence, who through a small group of his colleagues who remained in Prague continued to maintain contact with the Czech underground and with his former intelligence sources.

Even after March 15, 1939, when Hitler broke the Munich Pact and occupied all of Czechoslovakia, the West remained carefully neutral and would not recognize the Benes government, nor would it help or encourage Czech resistance of any sort.

From the day of the invasion, Czechs spent a great deal of time listening to their radios. What they listened for was a declaration of war against Germany by England and France; they heard instead a series of dicta from the invaders about their own destiny.

One of the first acts of the occupiers was to close down the universities. Slavs, deemed racially inferior to Aryans, were not considered educable; too much schooling would only make them dangerous; young men of hooligan age must be kept from congregating. Nevertheless these hooligans did congregate; during the first weeks there were demonstrations, many students were shot, 3,000 were arrested and sent to concentration camps. Karel Bergmann was one of these; he was sent to Oranienburg in Germany and later to Dachau, where eventually he died.

High schools were reopened on March 16, but Jews were forbidden to attend. All branches of the Sokol were immediately shut down; to assemble was *verboten*. All males between nineteen and forty had to register for duty in German labor camps; political activists, especially the Communist Party, went immediately underground.

Listening to foreign broadcasts also was forced underground. All Czechs were required to remove and give to the Gestapo the short-wave component of their radios which made foreign broadcasts accessible. The penalty for having this component in one's possession was immediate death. Nevertheless, those few components which were hidden and retained were precious possessions, carefully hoarded and carefully used for listening in secret to foreign news, especially the Czech-language broadcasts of the BBC.

But the radio brought little comfort and less information. It was mostly by word of mouth, often in the form of bitter jokes, that Czechs learned what was happening to their neighbors, their friends, their former colleagues, their country. During this uncertain period many young men, most of them students and former soldiers, crossed the borders illegally, hoping to form or to join independent brigades and fight for Czechoslovakia. Many made their way to England to join the struggling, still unrecognized, Czechosolvak Free Forces; some escaped through Poland, heading for Russia. Among the latter was Major Ludwik Svoboda.

During this period, although England remained aloof from the Czech resistance, Russia was helping. Funds for escape and materiel were made available through Yugoslavia and through the Communist underground. Major Svoboda and others were able to reach Russia, where he organized the underground transport of many soldiers out of Czechoslovakia to Russia and France. But in August 1939, when Russia stunned the world by signing a non-aggression pact with Germany, Major Svoboda's budding Czech Brigade was trapped in the Soviet Union, now no longer an ally. The entire brigade was rounded up and interned.

Armed with Russia's promise to keep hands off, Germany attacked Poland a week later, on September 1. On September 3, England honored its pact with Poland and declared war, France declared war, and World War II was unleashed. This gave the Czechoslovak Free Forces in France and England and the government-in-exile in London a new status: Czech pilots were accepted in the R.A.F., some Czechs joined the British Eighth Army, and the Czechoslovak Brigade in England was encouraged while its Russian counterpart chafed in prison.

A resistance movement in the homeland also developed right after the invasion. Cut off from the customary, natural methods of communication and congregation, each man, each woman, each boy and girl was utterly alone in making decisions and forming judgments. With no clear, dependable information reaching Prague, with our "allies" changing from day to day, it was not easy either to serve or to avoid disservice. German methods of interrogation made it unwise—*unhelpful*—to know what, if anything, was happening. Those who worked were reluctant to endanger others or to trust others with information. A Czech would therefore in the course of a normal day be faced with a sudden, spot decision about some act or lack of action the background or consequences of which he knew nothing. He would act or not act on the basis of his own inner makeup, instinct, sympathies, experience, or sudden judgment. He might never know if he had acted rightly or wrongly or if, indeed, there had in truth been anything to act rightly or wrongly about.

Despite these difficulties, a movement took shape. The leading groups were UVOD (Central Committee for the Homeland Resistance) and the Communist underground. Due perhaps to the precarious support given both of these groups by their outside political allies, they cooperated with each other throughout the occupation, although they sometimes disagreed. Thus Czechoslovakia was spared the fratricide that existed in Poland and Yugoslavia.

Within UVOD, and working closely together, were the National Defense (made up of Czech officers and soldiers) and OSVO (Sokol in Resistance). In retrospect these organizations seem organized and widespread and they appear formidable in German documents and lists of executions. At the time of the unfolding of this story, we meet a few of their members, one by one.

Among the officers who had elected to remain in the homeland and organize acts of sabotage were Lieutenant-Colonel Josef Masin and Major Vaclav Moravek. These two, with the assistance of a radio operator named Yaroslav Peltan, had undertaken to maintain secret radio contact with General Bartik in London and with his counterpart in Moscow, also to keep in touch with valuable intelligence sources which were still in Czechoslovakia.

Chief among these was an already legendary figure known to the underground only by his code name, Franta (Czech for Frank). His real name and personality, and his cover identity, were known only to the very few directly concerned, nor did anyone except the Germans care to identify him. Franta had been feeding information to General Bartik long before the Munich Pact—since 1936, to be exact. At that time, as A-54, he was a paid agent of the Czechoslovak Army High Command.

During 1938 he informed Czech military authorities about a secret radio network, built by German Military Intelligence, on Czechoslovak territory. This was to be used, as a similar device was later used in Poland, to foster an "incident" in Czechoslovakia, giving Germans an excuse to attack. The knowledge of this network and foreknowledge of the plan were crucial to the maintenance of Czech unity during the crisis. Franta's advance intelligence of Germany's planned invasion on March 15, 1939, enabled many Czech leaders to leave the country just under the wire. General Bartik and the High Command trusted Franta's information implicitly, depended on it, and were eager to assure its continuing availability.

After the occupation, the army was of course no longer recognized, and officers were assigned by the German "protectors" to various civilian jobs. Lieutenant-Colonel Masin's disciplined personality enabled him, despite the tense nature of his undercover activities, to climb meekly to a bookkeeper's stool and maintain an obedient façade, although this must have been extremely difficult. Major Moravek, however, could not physically or mentally resign himself to his clerical work. An active, dynamic career soldier in his early thirties, he preferred to live in constant danger rather than to keep books submissively. He therefore disappeared but stayed in Prague, living underground twenty-four hours a day.

Another who could not go on with daily life while his country was in deep trouble was a middle-aged Moravian professor of chemistry named Ladislav Vanek.

Vanek's wife was also a teacher in Moravia. Feeling that she and their two children could manage to live in comparative safety if he did not involve them, he abruptly left home, telling her nothing. Shortly thereafter a retired invalid, wearing a moustache, inconspicuously appeared in Prague and quietly contacted some of his former Sokol associates.

On the surface, however, most people carried on in their assigned or accustomed jobs, outwardly obeying rules and subduing or repressing their defiance. Resistance, in the main, smoldered privately in each person. But every so often a spark from the deeply buried underground would touch, even burn, an ordinary individual.

Through the resourceful Franta and through the underground transmitter maintained by Colonel Masin, Major Moravek, and Sergeant Peltan, the Czechoslovak government-in-exile received advance warning of the attack on Poland. Details of the preliminary "incident" and the scheduled take-over of the Free City of Danzig, as well as information on planned troop movements, were transmitted to General Bartik. All of this information was passed to the British government, in June of 1939, by the still unrecognized Czechs.

The staging of the Polish incident was designed and directed by Hitler's top hatchetman, SS General Reinhard Heydrich. This talented troublemaker had also engineered the Czechoslovak preliminaries. Outstanding for his ruthlessness even among the German High Command, Heydrich had been selected to spearhead each forward thrust with a wedge of carefully planned subversion, division, and fratricide.

In Hitler's already formulated plans (as published in his book, *Mein Kampf*) the Slavic subjugation included all of Russia and led step by step to that ultimate goal. However, he was not yet ready to antagonize the Soviet Union and thereby risk a two-front war. The actual attack on Poland had to wait until the Russo-German non-aggression pact had been completed; but the groundwork had been prepared by Heydrich long before that day in August when Stalin embraced his new ally.

In the spring of 1939, SS General Heydrich hand-picked from German prisons a collection of "pure Aryan" convicts who were serving criminal sentences. He outfitted these trusties with Polish uniforms, drilled them in specific techniques, and at the proper moment set them to attack the German radio station at Gleiwitz on the Polish border. This Polish outrage against innocent Germans unleashed anguished howls of Hitlerian propaganda against Poland; promptly on cue, his vengeful armies thundered into Poland to avenge the outrage—forcing France and England into the war. The Czechoslovak *émigrés* in these two countries were now officially recognized as a government-in-exile.

At this time General Josef Palecheck, formerly of the air force in Czechoslovakia, organized a group of paratroopers who were to return to the homeland to perform acts of sabotage against the Germans. All of these young men were former soldiers in the Czech Army who had escaped to England in order to serve in just this way. As part of the Special Forces of the Czechoslovak Intelligence, they were trained in commando tactics along with British commandos in dour woodlands surrounding the battlements of a grim Scottish castle.

Meanwhile SS Obergruppenfuhrer Reinhard Heydrich moved on to his next scheduled task: to slip a blindfold on Yugoslavia and get that country ready for the noose.

Escape

My father had remained in Yugoslavia during the period when our allies maintained their neutrality and he had been able to rent a tiny house in the north of that country. My mother urged me to join him there.

She and I had not as yet been seriously molested, and we had many Czech friends; but our position was ambiguous. As Jews, we had no legitimate activities. I continued my studies with the help of Vlasta Chervinka, who brought me my assignments and explained the new work. But I could not attend school. Before the occupation, my mother had been active with the Committee to Help Anti-Nazi Refugees, a group which had spirited many people out of Germany. Through her connections she obtained a false passport for me and insisted that I escape.

As I mentioned, there were difficult decisions to make in those days. This was one of them. I was afraid to go, afraid to stay. I was reluctant to desert my mother, my country, my friends; but I could not help them by staying, and any day I might be arrested on some pretext or other. There was the chance, if I got through, that I could join a Czech brigade. There was also the strong chance that I would not get through. This is the sort of private turmoil each decision evoked, sometimes with only ten seconds in which to resolve it.

In the end I went. Vlasta helped me to get ready. He kept a conversation going, while I packed, to keep my mother from tears. To prove to both of us that he would visit her often and keep an eye on her, he set aside my discarded belongings in separate piles, describing his plans for each of them. My boots and my old trousers would fit a disadvantged friend. This got my mother to start finding uses for my things among her committee friends. By the time I was ready to leave, she and Vlasta were mock-fighting over whose friends should have my warm ski jacket.

Knowing the problems of refugees, my mother gave me her gold necklace to use for money or for a bribe when needed. I boarded the streetcar across the road to travel to the station, and she stood at the window and waved goodbye, still dry-eyed and active. That picture framed itself in my memory.

The false travel permit allowed me to cross the border by train into Austria, which was also German-occupied. In Vienna I had to change trains. I traveled across the city from the Westbahn Station to the Sudbahn Station, where trains left for Yugoslavia via the Semmering. Although this happened without adventure, it was very tense. I still remember how it all felt; I rode in a compartment with two ladies who were wives of German officers. They chatted with enthusiasm about the victories in Poland, in which their husbands had taken part. They discussed with absolute confidence their husbands' future duties in France and in Great Britain. I pretended not to understand the German language.

We approached the border, and the customs officers and Gestapo men boarded the train in the town of Graz. I had to open all my luggage. The Gestapo threw everything out and inspected each article minutely. Even my toothpaste was cut to pieces, to be sure that nothing was hidden in it. I had to give them my mother's gold necklace, and then they let me cross the border.

When I found myself actually in Yugoslavia and heard the border guards speaking a language so similar to Czech, I felt a great relief. In only six months I had forgotten the feeling of freedom. I traveled through this very different world, very conscious of the difference, to northern Yugoslavia. My father met me in Lublyana.

In Prague my father had been in the business of importing and exporting goods from the neighboring countries, so he had contacts. He also had sufficient money. In his little house we waited for a permit to enter Great Britain.

This had been promised, so we expected it daily. We also hoped that my mother would be able to arrange her own escape. While we waited, we played chess and listened to the radio. Each evening we went to dinner at a nearby restaurant-hotel where my father, who could speak English, interpreted the BBC. broadcasts for anyone who was interested. Each evening a small crowd awaited our arrival, hoping that this time we would bring good news. Instead my father had to tell these people about Denmark, about Norway, about Holland and Belgium.

France and England were awaiting Germany at the Maginot Line.

Resistance

A "Reichsprotector of Bohemia and Moravia" had been established in Prague to oversee the occupation. This gentleman, Freiherr von Neurath, settled into Hradcañy Castle, delegated responsibility, and gave hunting and dinner parties attended by upper-crust Germans and Czech collaborators. A Prussian aristocrat, von Neurath saw his duties as administrative and diplomatic; therefore he limited his contacts as much as possible to ministers of the Protectorate Government and to important industrialists.

Direct dealings with the conquered populace were left to von Neurath's state secretary, Karl Hermann Frank. This dignitary, a Sudeten German known to the Czechs as "K. H." (pronounced, in that language, *Kah Hah*), disliked his superior's nonchalance. He lacked the authority to influence Gestapo tactics but felt that the growing incidence of Czech sabotage should be better controlled. Accordingly he decided to prepare a secret, documented report for Adolf Hitler, detailing von Neurath's "incompetence in the face of Czech arrogance" and hinting that this charming figurehead should be replaced by someone of sterner mold. There is no doubt that K. H. conceived himself to be the obvious replacement.

Conspicuous acts of sabotage at that time were almost exclusively the province of Colonel Masin and Major Moravek. At every opportunity one or the other would blow up a train or a bridge. A small cache of explosives was maintained for them near a dynamite factory in Pardubice from which they were systematically stolen by one or more workers. When an occasion arose, such as a movement of German troops or supplies, Masin or Moravek would go to Pardubice and collect the equipment they needed.

Returning to Prague from one such errand, Moravek traveled by train with his explosives in a bulky suitcase. An unexpected Gestapo patrol boarded his railway car to make a sudden spot-check. Before they reached his compartment, and while they were still checking luggage and asking questions in the next section, he managed to lower his suitcase through the window, using his belt. As gently as he could, he deposited his loaded luggage on the bank beside the moving train—then held his breath, expecting to be blown up at any moment. Hearing no explosion, he relaxed, blandly displayed his false papers and answered questions, then got off at the next station.

He borrowed a wheelbarrow from the station-master (no questions asked or answered). He trundled this along the tracks until he found his precious suitcase. He wheeled it back, returned the barrow, and boarded the very next train which came along. On this one he was able to complete his journey, take his cargo to its planned destination, and complete his mission on schedule.

Needless to say, each obvious act of sabotage against the Germans cheered and heartened the Czech people as much as it annoyed their conquerors. There was little enough in Czech daily life which could bring cheer. The German-controlled radio brayed news of victory after victory; these reports were confirmed by the BBC, listened to in secret at the risk of death. Food was rationed. Work was assigned. Gatherings and customary activities were forbidden. Young men were sent to Germany to forced labor; others disappeared. Many people were arrested. Some however kept from having any involvement or curiosity.

Explosions were visible to all. An "accident" to a train could not go unnoticed. Each sign of resistance was a matter of great importance to the Czech people. K. H., increasingly distressed, lengthened his "little list." The chief of the Prague Gestapo, Otto Geschke, was stirred to appoint a special deputy, Police Captain Oskar Fleischer, to concentrate on hunting down the saboteurs.

Although Masin's activities were not suspected, it was not long before Fleischer identified his quarry as the missing bookkeeper, former major of the Czech Army, Vaclav Moravek. All of Moravek's former colleagues denied remembering what he looked like, but army files in German custody produced a photograph and statistics. An intense hunt for Moravek was begun. Oskar Fleischer had caught the scent and was hot on the trail.

Major Moravek had seemingly superhuman courage and a bizarre sense of humor. The thought of having his own personal German police dog in hot pursuit intrigued and challenged him. He lost no chance to tease and heckle his pursuer, leaving false clues and rude messages.

However, by the spring of 1940 Fleischer had unearthed his hiding place and Moravek was forced to move. In his haste he left a few belongings, including his winter coat. To punish Fleischer for causing him inconvenience, he addressed a letter to Fleischer's boss, Geschke, asking him to forward it. Postmarked Bratislava, it read, "Dear Otto: I had to leave for warmer regions because you stole my winter coat. Furthermore, I don't feel secure under the protection of the Great German Reich." It was boldly signed Vaclav Moravek.

Simultaneously a postcard also addressed to Geschke arrived from Belgrade. In this one Moravek crowed that on a Prague street, on a certain day, he had asked Fleischer for a light for his cigarette. Fleischer had "very kindly" given him a light from his own cigar "without recognition, only with courtesy." Moravek was doubly grateful since he had done this on a bet (with Masin) of one thousand crowns, and he could now buy a new winter coat.

Fleischer was furious. Not only was he hauled on the carpet by his boss, but all of Prague, including his Gestapo colleagues, found the incident amusing. Seeing Moravek in every passerby, he arrested a series of youngish, balding men of wiry build, submitted them to a grueling interrogation, and released each one only after he was proved beyond a doubt to be someone other than Fleischer's quarry.

Since each non-Moravek arrested made him look more foolish, Fleischer was forced to relinquish this tactic and outwardly to calm down. At about this time the dauntless major chose to heckle him again. One morning a scrawled message in Czech appeared on a wall inside Gestapo Headquarters: "Wanted to introduce myself to Fleischer during office hours, Fleischer absent, sorry can't wait, have to blow up a train—Vaclav Moravek!"

This particular jest was enjoyed more by the Prague populace than by the Gestapo. A renewal of the relentless ferreting by Fleischer's men turned up the latest hiding place, and this time Fleischer himself led the outsized band of men which crept up to surround the building. Presumably only the Gestapo knew that the raid was planned; nevertheless a warning reached Moravek in time for him to get away.

When the door of the hideout was battered down, the premises were found to have been vacated—winter coat and all. A lone table in the center of the single room bore a heap of excrement. This substance held a note, upright, which read, "Oskar, sorry to disappoint you but this is the only part of myself I leave to you. Enjoy this modest gift. Give it to the Winterhilfe (a Nazi charity organization) —Moravek."

Despite the games Moravek played in his lighter moments, his specific, very strategic duty was to maintain contact with Intelligence Agent A-54, code name "Franta." At this time Moravek was the only member of the Prague underground entrusted by General Bartik with the knowledge of this man's cover identity. Moravek was Franta's contact; he and Masin, along with Peltan, decoded Franta's messages, recoded them for transmission, then dispatched them promptly to General Bartik in London. Although occasionally side-tracked for purposes of sabotage, and by Moravek's personal vendetta with Oskar Fleischer, the team kept its transmitter humming with information as fast as Franta could provide it.

In April 1940, a month before France was invaded, an urgent message was hurriedly dispatched describing German plans to attack France. Details of the planned Rochade march along the Maginot Line, with a push by German troops from Belgium, were described minutely. This intelligence was received with great excitement by the Czechs in London and was transported immediately by personal courier to the French General Staff. However, although the French knew of the reliability of information from Czech sources, they were convinced of the impregnability of their Maginot Line. They did not believe that this type of attack was either probable or feasible, and did nothing to offset it. A few weeks later France fell—having been attacked by exactly the method Franta had described.

In Prague, news of France's downfall was blared enthusiastically by the German radio all through the day and evening. Simultaneously the Czechs who still had the cherished shortwave radio component listened almost continuously to the news of Churchill's determined stand.

This shortwave gadget was now fairly common in homemade form, contrived by those who knew the insides of a radio. It was never sold but was presented as a prized Christmas present, or birthday present, to trusted friends or relatives. Promptly nicknamed *churchillky* it enabled thousands of Czechs to be heartened by Churchill's promise to "fight on from the beaches . . . to fight on from Canada, if necessary."

Through churchillky Czechs heard about the Free French forces under De Gaulle which were forming in Canada; through the German radio they heard about the entry of Italy into the war. Slavs, however, were not impressed either by French resistance or Italian perfidy. Their hope and faith were pinned on England and the United States. Nor were they fooled by the Russo-German Pact; they confidently awaited the day when Hitler would attack Russia, which would then again become their strong ally.

To the underground team of men who had daily risked their lives to warn France of the coming invasion, the complete bypassing of their warning was a discouraging setback. For Moravek, the only outlet was to intensify his sabotage activities and confound Fleischer. Franta, however, kept the information coming; Bartik sent messages of encouragement; and the team settled back into its routine job of decoding and transmitting.

At the end of July 1940, Franta again had important information, this time about Hitler's plans for England. During the next several weeks complete plans for an invasion, scheduled for September 15, were dispatched to London. Ships, fast boats, submarines, and aircraft spreading poison gas were to be used. On the basis of these reports, supplemented and confirmed by other sources, England was able to arrange defenses which forced Germany to abandon this invasion strategy and resort instead to attacks from the air.

The usefulness and timeliness of intelligence from the Czech sources was acknowledged by the British government. At this time Winston Churchill and other representatives thanked the government-in-exile for "helping Britain in her most critical times." This message of thanks was transmitted to the Prague team by General Bartik through their underground communication system.

By the end of that September, Franta notified the Czech resistance that Hitler had abandoned his intention of invading England and was working feverishly at a strategy called *Barbarossa*. This was a plan for imminent attack on the Soviet Union. To prepare for this, Reinhard Heydrich had set the fuses for "alliances" with Hungary, Rumania, and Bulgaria. He expected to do the same with Yugoslavia, whose regent, Paul, was already in Hitler's camp. But Heydrich had created special shock troops, which had already been planted and were set to go into action if Yugoslavia dragged its feet.

Within Yugoslavia two groups were easily susceptible to Nazi propaganda. One was the small German minority, which fell snugly into line with the usual arguments of Aryan supremacy. The other was the *Ustashi*—a fanatically separatist organization within Roman Catholic Croatia. These Ustashi were mostly illiterate, highly emotional people who resented the supremacy of Orthodox Catholic Serbia and admired Hitler. Resentment was easily fomented into fear and hatred by Heydrich's "diplomats," who also provided the Ustashi with arms and ammunition to be used in a frenzied massacre of Serbians, carefully timed to come to a boil at a moment that would coincide with the German entry into Belgrade.

Complete details of these plans were discovered by Franta and sent by Moravek to Czech Intelligence in London. General Bartik forwarded the information to Paul of Yugoslavia immediately, in ample time for the Heydrich coup to be forestalled. But Paul, in Hitler's pocket, promptly sent the report and news of its source to his new Führer. When Paul's government was overthrown by patriots of the Yugoslav Army—who presumably would have used the information to preserve their country's unity—the report was safely in Germany and Heydrich's shock troops went into unsuspected, unhampered action.

Needless to say, the German High Command had already become uncomfortably aware of an important intelligence leak which had weakened many of its strategies. News that the source was Czechoslovakian reached Hitler at the same time as K. H. Frank's report on von Neurath's incompetence. As soon as Heydrich's job in the Balkan corridor, culminating in the Ustashi slaughter of their Serbian neighbors, had been wrapped up, "Hitler's Hangman" was urgently dispatched to the newly located, high-priority trouble spot—Prague.

His assignment was to stamp out resistance, *Germanize* the Czechs, and *get Franta.*

Game of Chess

In Yugoslavia my father and I continued to await the papers which would get us to England.

We also still hoped for my mother's escape. While we we're living in our house near Lublyana we received two censored letters from her. These told us that she had "given" her nice apartment to a German Air Force colonel, including all the furniture and household equipment, which she no longer needed. She was now living in a single room which had been "found" for her. This was in Old Town, near the Karel Boromeo (Orthodox) Church, in an apartment shared by several families, all Jewish. Places were being "found" for Jews in this part of the city.

My friend Vlasta still lived in the same place in the old neighborhood. He visited her often, bringing pastries or other special treats which his mother had made. My mother was not clever about making her ration last.

She made no mention, of course, of any plan of joining us. We pored over her letters for between-the-lines communication but found little to encourage us except the fact that she had not been arrested. A letter from Vlasta, also censored, told me only that my mother was well and cheerful and that he was keeping an eye on her. Eva Fisher, his fiancée, had also moved with her family to Old Town, so he went there often. He would graduate from high school soon, and that summer would start working as an office boy in the Barandov Film Studios.

I was able to extract a little hope from Vlasta's letter. The word *cheerful* might mean that my mother still had her contacts, was still planning to escape.

Vlasta was passionately patriotic. He was also a confirmed Anglophile and maintained a strong conviction that England would come through to stop the Germans. An innate belief in justice and nonviolence had aroused his hatred for the Hitler regime long before it reached out to distort his own life. Despite his nonviolent convictions he *had* volunteered for army service during the general mobilization. However, a serious childhood illness had left him too frail to pass the physical examination, so he had not been a soldier.

Although physically not up to army standards, he was active and athletic. A good dresser, with curly blond hair, he could present an outward appearance of the perfect office boy. But I knew him as a scholar, a thinker, a student of languages, a faithful Sokol member. I assumed he would be doing what he could for the resistance, in one form or another.

With Vlasta looking after my mother, I could reasonably maintain a hope of seeing her in Yugoslavia, probably accompanied by his Jewish fiancée. Fortified by the optimism I had managed to squeeze from this short letter, I continued to play chess with my father and to accompany him each evening to the restaurant for his nightly translation of the BBC broadcast.

Like the Yugoslavs among whom we lived, my father had little faith in France's ability to hold out but was convinced that England, backed by America, would never be beaten. It was his belief that Hitler was "winning himself to death." He was sure that, like Napoleon, Hitler would ultimately attack Russia, spread himself too thin, and bring about his own downfall.

Fervent discussions on the progress of the war followed each news broadcast. At this small restaurant—as doubtless all over the world—the pawns, while waiting to be moved, played "armchair general."

The news of the fall of France—in Lublyana, at least—was offset by the immediate entry of England into active participation. On the same evening that the news of France reached us, it was my father's dramatic duty to translate Winston Churchill's "blood, sweat, and tears" speech to his regular listeners. Himself deeply moved and excited by the passionate words, he conveyed all of Churchill's conviction and determination to his eager audience. His own renewed hope, faith, and courage were equal to theirs. Among that gathering, larger than usual since news of a special occasion had spread quickly, Churchill's speech, translated by my father, was accepted as the certain beginning of Hitler's end.

The permit to enter England finally reached us, but it was too late. On Easter Sunday, 1941, the Germans attacked Belgrade from the air and at the same time, in a pincer movement, their armies from Rumania and Bulgaria probed the borders of Yugoslavia. With many others my father and I tried to escape; but as we hurried toward the railway station amid the stream of refugees, our town was attacked by German Air Force Stukka dive bombers. We were pressed into the throng of people in the main square.

Everyone outdoors was trapped. The local householders had locked and blocked their doors in fear of looting. The main square was full of loyal Yugoslav soldiers, barefoot, with their cannons and wagons drawn by oxen and cows, unable to move backward or forward and of course helpless against the planes. When the attack occurred, dozens of soldiers and civilians were killed by machine gun fire, by bombs, or were trampled to death. My father and I were in the middle of this melee waiting to be killed, but nothing happened to us.

When the attack ceased, we went back to our house. We had not been harmed, but I noticed after that experience that a change had come over my father. Formerly energetic and enterprising, he was now apathetic and depressed. He seemed to have lost all hope of getting out of this encirclement.

From then on we stayed indoors, always listening for the pounding on the door which would mean that the Gestapo had found us. One day as we were playing chess—in which, out of habit, my father still excelled—he abandoned even this pretense at occupation. He pushed the board away and stood up.

"Jan," he said, "I have made a decision."

Curious, I waited.

"I have thought about our situation," he said. "I have come to the conclusion that it is hopeless. We are waiting only for the Gestapo, who will ship us to Germany, where we will be sent to a concentration camp and exposed to much humiliation. I don't want to give the Nazis that pleasure.

"Tonight I will take the only way out—I will commit suicide. My mind is made up. But I am worried about leaving you. I sincerely believe that your situation also is hopeless. It would be a great relief to me if you would join me—but the decision is up to you."

At twenty years of age it is not natural to accept any situation as hopeless. I thought we should at least try to escape and, if we must, die trying. I thought of my mother in Prague— still alive, doubtless buoyed up by her hopes for my safety.

I told my father that I would like to try to run away, and urged him to try too.

His own decision was firm, but he gave me all the money he had and the address of a friend in Lublyana and that of another friend in Italy. He advised me to try to reach Italy, as the Italians were much milder in their treatment of prisoners than were the Germans. If I could reach Italy, or Italian-occupied territory, he believed I had a chance.

That evening we sat as usual and played chess together. My father smoked a cigarette, and when it was finished he stood up and looked at me.

"So now," he said, "we have to say goodbye to each other. Please promise to stay with me until I am dead. It would be horrible if I were taken to a hospital, my stomach pumped out, and I should live to be humiliated and die a more terrible death in a concentration camp."

Knowing my father, I could understand that he dreaded humiliation and torture more than death. I promised. He gave me three sleeping pills and watched me take them. Then we embraced and said goodbye, and I went to my room. I lay down on my bed—and all at once the terror of the situation hit me. I jumped out of bed and ran into my father's room, where he was measuring some white powder onto a piece of paper.

"You must not disturb me again," he said, firmly pushing me out. Already drowsy from the pills, I stumbled back to my own room and fell asleep.

In the morning as soon as I awoke I ran into his room again and saw him deeply unconscious and breathing heavily, very red in the face. I called him and shook him, but he did not respond.

All at once a great panic took hold of me. I felt completely alone, completely helpless. I do not remember how long this moment lasted, but for a second or two I too considered suicide.

I remembered how tired my father had seemed, and how much trouble he had known during his life. I did not want to live to be constantly persecuted. But I also remembered that my father had known many good things.

I was only twenty. I could not accept the thought of killing myself when I had not yet lived. I was too young. I was not yet tired enough to surrender the future without a fight. The moment passed. Nevertheless, dazed with grief, fear and confusion, I sat with my father for about four hours—long after he had stopped breathing.

I stayed in the house, drifting aimlessly from room to room, until night fell. Then I took the money and addresses he had given me, jumped out the window into the back yard, and ran across the corn fields as fast as I could toward the railway line that led to Lublyana. After a short time a freight passed, moving slowly, and I was able to jump on and hide beneath the iron steps of the last car.

In Lublyana I spent the rest of the night sitting on a park bench, and in the morning I went to see my father's friend. He gave me money but would not let me into his house. Although the town was occupied by the Italian Army, he said, it was full of Gestapo. He urged me to forget his address and not to mention his name.

By that time I was exhausted. I decided to travel by train to the Italian border, but I desperately needed a night's sleep. So I went to the largest hotel in Lublyana and booked a room.

I had no trouble getting a room, but after I was in it I heard a series of German conversations in the corridor. I realized that the hotel was—logically—full of Gestapo. So I again passed a night without sleeping, sitting in a chair by the window, ready to slide down the drainpipe at as much as a knock on the door. Nothing happened, and toward morning I fell asleep in my chair and slept most of the day.

When I awoke I went to the railway station and without any difficulty took a train for a border town on the Sava River. I arrived there late in the evening, waited for nightfall, then swam across the river to Italian territory.

Wet and chilled, I stumbled into the nearby forest and fell asleep. By walking at nighttime and sleeping and hiding during the day, I managed to cover the hundred kilometers from the border to Trieste in a week or so. However, once I had succeeded in reaching Trieste I had no plan. My father's friend was in Genoa, but to reach Genoa I would have to cross all of northern Italy. I did not look forward to walking such a distance, and I was afraid to travel by train as in Italy there were probably frequent police checkups. I was also not sure that my father's friend would help me.

Drifting without a destination down the main street, I noticed a dairy shop with a Slovenian name over the door. I had money, so I went into this store and bought some milk, bread, and cheese. I talked to the owner while I ate (Slovenian is very like Czech); and since I was now too exhausted to be cautious or even to care what happened, I took a desperate chance and confided in him. This Slovenian shopkeeper let me stay in his back room for a whole week, resting and eating, while we considered what I should do next.

Heydrich's Assignment

Living underground in an occupied country is a complicated matter. Professor Ladislav Vanek, having left his family and his teacher's salary behind him in Moravia, needed an income in Prague and a place to live. His old friend, Professor Jan Zelenka, was able to solve his problem.

Zelenka's ingenuity, his wide acquaintanceship in Prague, and his intuitive ability to trust the right people soon made him the unofficial quartermaster of the resistance movement. During years of teaching class after class of chemistry students, he had come to know not only his students but their families. It was said of him that he "never lost a pupil, only gained a friend."

In a very short time he was able to provide Vanek with an identity, a residence, and an income—while also providing two other workers with a means of support. For a small consideration—enough to pay board to a family in lean circumstances—Professor Vanek presented himself once a week to the proper authorities as the husband of a Mrs. Alesh. In this way he collected the pension check due the real Mr. Alesh, who had recently died. He shared this with the widow Alesh, enabling her to continue her activities, then paid the rest in the form of rent to still a third family of patriots.

This chore performed, Vanek was free to sun himself on a park bench for the sake of his newly acquired tuberculosis. His needs beyond room and board were limited to keeping a small supply of 25-heller pieces on hand for use in making occasional social phone calls. These were made in a public booth—often after a certain youngish, balding, debonair fellow had sauntered out of the same booth having just completed a call of his own.

On such an occasion in August of 1941, the note which Moravek left for "Jindra" (cover name for Ladislav Vanek) informed him in their private code that London wanted an important German assassinated on the Czechoslovakian National Holiday, October 28. This dramatic act would show the Western world that the Czechs were still resisting, and that the West could count on internal help from the people of Czechoslovakia.

Moravek's own suggested target was K. H. Frank. Did Vanek agree?

Moravek was gleeful about this project, as he himself had transmitted the idea to General Bartik as early as September 1939. He was eager to perform the task himself, but his suggestion had received no enthusiasm—until now.

Vanek's own talent for strategy, combined with his full-time availability, had soon caused him to inherit the leadership of the Prague underground. It was his frequent duty to tone down Major Moravek's love of reckless behavior. Although requests from the government in exile were usually accepted as orders, he regarded Moravek as far too valuable to allow him to take the risk of killing K. H. Frank. He also feared possible reprisals on the general Czech population which would severely damage the resistance organization.

To stall for time, Jindra (cover name for Vanek) composed a message to London requesting that the government in exile reconsider its decision. He also urged that if the assassination were ordered special care be taken to select an auspicious moment both militarily and politically for the undertaking. Moravek transmitted this procrastination obediently, although reluctantly. During the time in which the project was discussed back and forth, by radio to and from London and in secret meetings in Prague, Hitler's Hangman Reinhard Heydrich arrived in town. The German controlled press published the following notice of the change in Reichsprotectors:

Prague, Sept. 27, 1941. The Reichsprotector in Bohemia and Moravia the Reichsminister Freiherr von Neurath has suggested to the Führer that he grant him a long-term leave to enable him to restore his shattered state of health. Because the present state of war demands a full-time effort in the office of the Reichsprotector, Dr. von Neurath has asked the Führer simultaneously to free him of his duties as Reichsprotector until his health is restored and to name a deputy for this period. Under these circumstances, the Führer could not but grant the Reichsprotector's request and has entrusted SS Obergruppenführer Reinhard Heydrich with the office of Reichsprotector in Bohemia and Moravia for the period of Reichsminister von Neurath's illness.

Heydrich lost no time in demonstrating the difference between a sickly Reichsprotector and a vigorous one. On the day of his arrival he established courts-martial in Prague (as the capital of Bohemia) and in Brno (as the capital of Moravia). These bodies proceeded to sentence Czechs in wholesale numbers to execution or to concentration camps. During his first week in office 163 people were sentenced to death and 718 to concentration camps. Only fourteen people who appeared before the court-martial were acquitted. During his second week he gained momentum: his report to Hitler dated October 11 states that "so far approximately 5,000 people have been arrested in Bohemia and Moravia."

Since the purpose of this savage campagn was to smash the resistance movement and to track down the security leak, every person arrested was subjected to intense interrogation of the sort for which the Nazis had by then become infamous. The coded messages transmitted to London at that time contained horrible details of the new regime's oppression. By October 3 the Czech government in London knew exactly who the target of assassination should be.

On that day a special meeting of the exiled Czechoslovak Ministry of National Defense was held in London, to which were invited two young paratroopers from General Palecheck's Czechoslovak Special Forces group. These two had volunteered for special tasks and had been trained specifically for such missions. At this meeting they were intensely briefed on the situation in Czechoslovakia and were asked to mark October 28 "by an action that would enter history. . ."

The plan as set forth on that day was for these two to be parachuted into occupied Bohemia on October 10. This would give them time to make contact with the underground and to lay the groundwork for their mission. Meanwhile the underground in Prague would gather the necessary information on Heydrich's daily activities to help them select the appropriate time and place for the assassination.

This plan, however, did not materialize on the appointed day. One of the young men was badly injured during a practice jump. Since no immediate, specially trained substitute was available, the other, Josef Gabchik, was grounded until a new teammate could be found for him.

Meanwhile, back in Prague, the interrogation of Heydrich's court-martialed prisoners was producing a name here, a bit of information there—each bringing the Gestapo nearer the true sources of underground activity. Moravek and his team were forced to move constantly, now abandoning spare equipment in each desperate shift instead of mere winter coats. One evening, with their transmitter set up hurriedly in Peltan's apartment, the three were engrossed in sending a message to London when a dog in the building started to bark. In those times a dog's bark was enough to alert them to serious danger. But their message was too urgent and their concentration too deep for the warning to penetrate. Not until the doorbell rang with the staccato, insistent Morse code of the Gestapo did they realize that they were trapped.

"I'll stall them!" Masin said. He jumped to the door, his hand on the pistol in his pocket, and started arguing with the unexpected callers to give the others a moment in which to work. Quickly Moravek and Peltan destroyed their intelligence material.

Forced to open the door, Masin shot the nearest Gestapo man in order to focus attention on himself. The Gestapo, interested in taking prisoners alive for interrogation, jumped him immediately instead of shooting back. In the ensuing fight Masin succeeded in steering the battle toward the top of the stairs and they all, including himself, rolled down in a bundle. His leg was caught in a bannister and broken; from his vantage point halfway down the stairs he emptied his pistol at his assailants, and then he was helpless.

But the time he had given to Moravek and Peltan enabled them to get away. Using a steel cable which was part of their quickly dismantled transmitter, they bound it to a sofa and dropped it from the apartment window, forty-five feet from the ground. Then they slid down themselves. Peltan's foot was badly injured; Moravek's left index finger was nearly cut off. Thrusting the bleeding hand into his pocket, he boarded a streetcar and rode for a short distance.

He hopped off near the home of his friend, Lydia Michova, in whose apartment he kept a spare transmitter.

She was not there, so he cared for his wound himself. With a razor blade he cut off the dangling finger, flushed it down the toilet, then wrapped his hand in a small, clean towel. After doing this, he wrote a note to Lydia apologizing for the bloodstains in the bathroom, took the spare transmitter, and left to seek a new sending station and to hunt for Peltan.

Moravek walked around Prague all night, avoiding the Gestapo while hoping to find his wireless operator. In the morning he visited another friend, a train conductor, who gave him breakfast.

Peltan was caught during that night. Both he and Masin were subjected to intensive German interrogation.

Twice during that week Major Moravek was nearly trapped. Although he managed to escape on both occasions, the last shreds of his equipment and all of his coding material fell into Gestapo hands. Without these he could no longer communicate with General Bartik in London.

The government in exile was frantic. Not only were they now out of touch with the Prague underground, but they had also lost the means of receiving the highly strategic communications of Intelligence Agent A-54, code name *Franta*. In a desperate attempt to re-establish radio contact with the homeland, they parachuted a radiotelegraph operator, with equipment and a new deciphering key, into Bohemia. This young man, Frantisek Pavelka, landed about eighty miles northeast of Prague on the night of October 3, 1941.

Although hurriedly assigned, he had been carefully briefed about the danger of his position. He had been provided with addresses of resistance workers who would hide him and his radio setup, and had been told to contact no one else. He knew that the Gestapo had discovered the identities, and therefore the relatives, of most of the Czech paratroopers who were training in Scotland. Nevertheless, instead of following his orders exactly he took time between communications to make daily visits to his family.

On October 25 he was arrested at a cousin's house, interrogated, and later executed. His equipment was also confiscated, his code key rendered useless.

Interrogation by Nazi methods, as everyone knows, was not a matter of questions asked and answered or not answered. Prisoners were interrogated until their responses were no longer intelligible. They were then given time for minimal recuperation and interrogated some more. All those who were even suspected of having any connection with the underground were subjected to particularly intense treatment—Colonel Masin, Sergeant Peltan, and Frantisek Pavelka among them. All three managed to die without disclosing information which would have been of much use to the Gestapo.

Although Pavelka's recklessness did not lead to the capture of other resistance workers, it gave the underground a bad scare. The next arrivals from England had to prove themselves thoroughly before their homeland contacts put them in touch with Major Moravek.

The next group with radiotelegraphic equipment was ready to fly to Bohemia on October 29—as soon as Pavelka's transmitter was known to have been silenced. However, a long stretch of extremely bad weather made it impossible for them to undertake the venture until late December. By that time another group, groomed for sabotage, was ready to leave, and a partner had been found to work with Josef Gabchik on the "action that would enter history," the assassination of Reinhard Heydrich.

Thus, the plane which left England on the night of December 24, 1941, carried seven tense young paratroopers, each trained for a specific task and each in his own way entrusted with a portion of the life blood of Czechoslovakia.

Secrecy was so intensely maintained that none of those on the plane had any inkling of the others' missions. Each group, until the last moment before departure, had expected to travel alone.

For convenience in keeping in touch with England, each group had a code name known only to its members. As the separate teams boarded the plane, they were given strict orders not to talk to anyone during the flight; therefore, although all of these paratroopers had trained together and knew each other well; their surprised greetings on seeing each other were limited to exchanges of "Hi!" and "Good luck!" Each naturally wondered about the others' assignments. But the relentless noise of the four-engined Halifax which carried them rapidly toward their separate responsibilities soon forced them into isolation, each with his own tense thoughts.

Since these young men were to land in occupied territory, and hopefully to look as though they belonged there, they were dressed in Czech-made civilian clothes. Care had been taken that all of their equipment, down to the chocolate bars and razor blades, should show no trace of English origin. They would drop into Bohemia during the night. In the morning, if they were seen, they would do their best to appear as though they had gone to bed in the normal manner the night before.

The first team dropped was "Anthropoid," the two men who were assigned to kill Heydrich. Over some fields outside of Prague, Josef Gabchik and his partner, Jan Kubish, jumped into the night. Their first task was survival, separately or together. Then to mingle with the landscape, then the crowd, then to find their way to the member of the underground who would provide them with a place to hide. The name and address they had memorized for this purpose was that of Professor Jan Zelenka.

Both Gabchik and Kubish had grown up in the country and had no relatives in Prague. There was no one in the vicinity whom they would risk their lives to visit; this advantage was offset by the fact that they were unfamiliar with the city. However, they were well equipped to mingle with the population unnoticed, both being typical, pleasant looking Czechoslovak young men of average build and height. Jan Kubish was the taller of the two, a bit heavier than Josef, quiet and friendly. Josef Gabchik was lean and lively, volatile but disciplined.

They were good friends. Both had been keyed up by the bad news from home which they had heard in England. Both were eager to punish Heydrich and put a stop to his ruthless persecutions. Landing separately, each made his way single-mindedly toward the appointed place, in accordance with their instructions.

The plane was over Pardubice when the next team jumped. This was "Silver A," the group which carried radio equipment and new codes and whose mission it was to re-establish contact with Moravek and Franta.

There were three men on this team: Lieutenant Alfred Bartos was entrusted with the leadership and with the codes; Jiri Potuchek, the radio operator, jumped with the transmitter; Josef Valchik was assigned to the special task of being radio contact for Anthropoid (Kubish and Gabchik) and keeping news of their progress, their needs, and/or their subsequent orders moving to and from London.

Resistance workers in Pardubice sheltered this group willingly; Potuchek's transmitter found a hiding place from which he could operate. But Bartos's task—to contact Major Moravek—was more difficult.

The organized chain of communication had been shattered by Heydrich's arrests, and those who knew Moravek's hiding place were not willing to divulge it. Two months passed before Bartos could break down this cautious reluctance, during which time, however, he and Potuchek established radio communication with London. It was in fact through London that contact with Moravek was finally made.

Mrs. Bocek, the wife of the Czech general of the army in exile, was still living in Prague and was actively supporting the resistance. Through Bartos's radio General Bocek in London sent a message to his wife in Prague, using a code known only to the two of them. Mrs. Bocek recognized the message as coming from her husband and therefore sanctioned by the London government. After taking thorough precautions to be sure that Bartos was indeed a paratrooper from England, and that the Gestapo was nowhere near his trail, she put him in touch with Major Moravek, thereby reopening the vital channel between London and Franta.

As soon as this contact was achieved, London radioed its thanks to Bartos, complimenting him on the "fearless, skillful, and well- planned procedure" which had enabled him to perform his chief mission.

By this time Major Moravek was no longer playing tricks on the Gestapo. The ruthless slaughter of his countrymen, the torture of his teammates, had forced him to share Professor Vanek's doubt of the advisability of the projected assassination. It was his feeling that time should be taken to reorganize the underground before they risked the possibility of newer, harsher repressions.

The five paratroopers who had managed to make contact provided valuable, trained new blood. Their addition to the core of the resistance gave the Prague underground new courage and vitality. A close cooperation developed between these five and Major Moravek (who still maintained the only contact with the intelligence agent Franta), and with Professor Vanek and his organization, with Zelenka and his contacts providing clothing, food, laundry, hiding places, and, when necessary, false identities.

The men in the third team, "Silver B," were too far from Prague when they parachuted from the English transport plane. Landing among country people, in whom caution was by nature deeply implanted, they were unable to make any contact with the resistance workers assigned to hide them. Too exposed to carry out their sabotage mission, and unable to reach equipment or information, they joined the guerrilla fighters in the mountains of Moravia.

Their failure to make contact was communicated by Bartos to the government in exile in London, which promptly started briefing other paratroopers to get ready to replace them.

Although Moravek was now against pulling off the assassination at that particular time, he was actively helping the determined Anthropoids, Kubish and Gabchik, to prepare the ground for carrying out their orders. He was entirely ready to play an important part in the deed himself. However, a new situation arose which demanded his full attention.

Somehow, although certainly not through the Prague underground or through any interrogation of Czechs, the Gestapo had begun to suspect Franta's cover identity.

Rails to Freedom

The Slovenian shopkeeper who befriended me in Trieste confirmed my suspicion that I would not be able to travel by train without a travel permit. He consulted some friends of his, and they advised that I stow away under a train, riding on an axle of the wheels of a fast express.

They explained in detail how I should do this. I should avoid a car directly behind the engine, because the engine would let off steam which would burn me. I should also avoid the end of the train, because the last few cars would have a lot of side to side motion and I would be nauseated. They advised a car in the midsection.

My benefactor took me to the station during the evening blackout and helped me to select the proper car on a train that was headed not only for Genoa but across the border into unoccupied France. We decided that, if possible, I should stay on the train into France and head for unoccupied Marseilles, where I knew that Czech officers had organized the transport of soldiers to the Czech brigades in North Africa and England. The axle of a car on a fast train is covered by a metal sheet to protect the wheels from the restrooms above. There is a crawl space between the floor of the car and this sheet, and that is where I established myself.

The ride was not too bad until, as we approached Venice, the train crossed a long bridge over the sea. It was very disturbing to look down from my precarious perch into the water far below. Also, although the sheet protected the wheels from the bathroom waste, it did not protect me; and as the trip lengthened, the passengers began to use the bathroom more frequently.

The rhythmical movement of the train made me very drowsy. I was afraid that I might fall asleep and fall off. So I bound myself to one of the upright bars, using my belt.

When the train reached Genoa, I watched the feet of the passengers descending from the train, then other feet ascending. I debated whether to get off too and try to reach my father's friend, but the possibility of reaching France was more tempting. I had been undisturbed so far, so I stayed where I was.

This soon appeared to be a mistake. A railway employee approached slowly from the last car, carrying a long-handled hammer. He was testing the steam in the brakes and inspecting the wheels for possible cracks. I watched him as he did his job conscientiously on each car, getting closer and closer to my hideout. Finally he reached the axle above which I was perched. He bent down to make his test—and our eyes met.

He said nothing. With no break in rhythm he continued his routine through the rest of the cars; then he left. I breathed easily again and thought good thoughts about this kind Italian workman who would help a refugee. But I was mistaken. In short order four high black boots appeared and stopped in front of my hiding place. I was dragged out and arrested.

A crowd gathered—of policemen, railway employees, and travelers—all Italian, a language I could not speak. They decided from my appearance that I was an English spy. Since I did not have the words to explain my real plight, I could not deny this and stood helpless while they shouted "Spio Inglese!" and spat at me, covering me with spittle.

I was handcuffed and taken to the Genoa Police Headquarters, where I was left alone for several suspenseful hours. During this time I relived the experiences with my father and the physical ordeal of the walk to Trieste and the ride under the train; by the time I was led to the office of the chief of police, I was in the grip of an uncontrollable trembling, the result of nerves and exhaustion.

This man spoke English. I had studied English at the Prague language school and was able to communicate with him. He seemed kind and fatherly. I poured out the whole story of my recent experiences; and he was sympathetic, even touched. There were tears in his eyes when I told him of my father's suicide.

He let me sit down until I calmed myself.

"I am sorry," he said, "but we will have to send you back to the German Protectorate of Bohemia and Moravia."

I could see that he really was sorry—but his regret did not comfort me.

"If you do that," I exploded, "it would be kinder and cheaper to shoot me right here! I will certainly be shot in Prague—and you will save all the money and the trouble of transporting me and feeding me!"

He thought this over. "All right," he said. "We'll give you a trial for illegally crossing the Italian border, and we'll see what comes of it."

I was sent to prison in Genoa. After three days I was tried and sentenced to nine months imprisonment and subsequent deportation to a prisoner of war camp in southern Italy. It may seem strange to have been delighted by such a sentence, but I was grateful and happy. I was tremendously relieved, because I dreaded the alternative—being sent back to German territory.

In prison I was treated as a political offender, not as a criminal. This meant that I was placed in solitary confinement, with a sign on my cell calling for maximum security. Since I had escaped from Yugoslavia, they expected me to try to escape again and did not plan to let that happen.

Once safely in jail, I had time to be miserable in solitary confinement. I had nothing to think about but my troubles, and nothing to read; the books in the prison library were all in Italian. I also had very little to eat. One day I was so hungry that I called the guard and, with my few Italian words, offered him my woolen sweater in exchange for food. He brought me some minestrone in my washbowl. I was so starved that I gulped it down—and was promptly tied in knots by a terrible stomach ache which lasted for hours and which was all I gained for the loss of my warm sweater.

The one break in my day was the exercise period during which, for half an hour, we were all marched around the prison yard in a circle under the eyes of guards with machine guns. This was at least in fresh air. The other prisoners talked to each other and played a finger game called *mona*, but since I did not know the language I could not join in or even converse with anyone.

One elderly prisoner sometimes smiled or nodded at me. One day he spoke to me in broken German—and I had found someone with whom I could communicate.

His name was Weinblut. He was a professional criminal but a very kind man. He was completely bald, rather stout, with steel-blue eyes; and he wore the kind of checkered felt slippers which proclaimed Central Europe. He could see that I was lonely in a foreign country and when I told him that I was kept in solitary confinement he offered to move into my cell with me.

"How could you manage that?" I asked him.

"No trouble!" he said. "No trouble at all. I have bribed all of the guards in this place."

Sure enough, the next day the door of my cell opened and Weinblut was ushered in, carrying his mattress, his blankets, and his washbowl. I was delighted to have his company. Since my cell had only one bed I gave it to him, put my own mattress on the floor, and helped him to get settled.

Franta and Moravek

Known only to Major Moravek, the German lawyer, Dr. Steinberg—playboy, social climber, frequenter of artistic, diplomatic, and government circles—was the Czech underground's most valued intelligence agent, A-54, called Franta.

Not long after Heydrich's arrival in Prague, Franta sensed that his cover identity was being investigated. His carefully maintained façade of frivolous activity seemed to be coming under more surveillance—by other than the husbands of his lady friends. He communicated this to Moravek, who turned all of his efforts toward helping his valued colleague.

Obviously in order to pursue his social activities in Prague circles, mingling with the Czech intelligentsia, the German lawyer, Dr. Steinberg, either had to have an airtight identity or use his smoke screen with Gestapo sanction. Again known only to Moravek, the latter was the case. To the Gestapo, and to the German High Command, Dr. Steinberg was the cover identity of Paul Thummel, chief of the German Military Intelligence for southeast Europe, stationed in Prague.

In this capacity he wore the Dr. Steinberg cover with full Gestapo sanction and cooperation, ostensibly as an important German agent. As a highly placed German agent he had access to secret, strategic German intelligence which, as A-54, he passed to the Allies through the Czech underground.

It has already been pointed out that in those days of sudden crisis—each man or woman made decisions alone, in terms of his own inner makeup. Who can analyze the private thoughts of young Paul Thummel, native of Saxony, son of a baker, who in 1936 decided to work under cover against Hitler? Here was this man who was trusted by the German inner circle. He was a personal friend of Hitler's close associate, Heinrich Himmler, Reichsleader of the SS. In fact, Thummel was even acquainted with the Führer himself. And yet, privately and quietly, he was working to promote the downfall of the Third Reich.

To the German Reich he would ultimately be a traitor. To the German people, loyal to the Reich, he would also be one. But to those few Germans who disapproved of Hitler's tactics but felt helpless to stop them, he would be a fool. To himself, perhaps, he was merely a member of the human race.

Those who now hear of the course he took during those dark days will make their own assessment. To those moved by blind patriotism: "My country, right or wrong," whatever the country—he was indeed a traitor. To those who place humanity first, Paul Thummel's singlehanded sabotage of the Hitler regime seems nothing but heroic. By accepting a strategic post in the Reich, he was always one step ahead of the coming barbarity, warning whomever was in the way to take cover.

The importance of his contribution can be measured by the passion with which he was hunted, and by the importance of the man who was pulled from other, highly sensitive tasks to lead the hunt. This was Reinhard Heydrich. And as Heydrich got closer to the source of the intelligence leak, agent A-54, Franta, found himself in danger. Disappearance into the Prague underground was impossible; this would confirm Dr. Steinberg's duplicity to the Germans. As Paul Thummel, he could be easily found. If this happened, it would also endanger any of the underground who had dared to hide or help him.

On the other hand, to the Prague underground, the German lawyer, Steinberg, was imagined by many as being an agent. But only Moravek knew that the playboy German was the legendary, indispensable A-54 who had direct access to German intelligence.

Moravek, racking his ingenious brain for a way to save Franta for future work and to protect Paul Thummel from being unmasked came up with a scheme whereby Dr. Steinberg would be kidnapped by the Prague underground and spirited out of the country, possibly with demands for ransom. A temporary haven in Switzerland, or some such neutral territory, must be found. To implement this plan, Moravek divulged Franta's identity to Vanek, Zelenka, and his paratrooper team, all of whom helped to lay the ground for this desperate solution.

Major Moravek's plot to rescue Franta by kidnapping Dr. Steinberg took temporary precedence over plans for assassinating Heydrich. But before details of the kidnapping could be worked out, Franta in his true identity as Paul Thummel received a summons from his German superiors to attend a conference of the Criminal Council of the Gestapo, to be held on February 22. His presence was urgently requested, as the conference was said to be most important.

Arriving there, he found that the meeting had been arranged for his own confrontation and arrest. SS Captain Abendschoen of the Gestapo, had undertaken to expose him. And he provided documents alleged to prove that Thummel was in contact with the hunted Major Moravek.

He was taken to Gestapo Headquarters in the nearby town of Kladno and submitted to several days and nights of intense, uninterrupted interrogation. During this time he insisted that his contact with Moravek had been carried on in pursuance of his own intelligence duties. He had tried, through Moravek, to penetrate the network of the Czech intelligence group to the real source of their information; he was getting closer and closer, but this stupid arrest had interrupted him at a most strategic point.

He admitted that he had kept his contact with Moravek a secret from his friend Oskar Fleischer. This was because Fleischer, for personal reasons, would have arrested Moravek too soon. He needed more time to trick Moravek into revealing his sources.

Abendschoen was half convinced—and half eager to believe. There was rivalry between Gestapo officers for the ripest plum; and if

Thummel could lead him to both Moravek and Franta he would not only trump Oskar Fleischer but would probably be in line for a promotion. He presented this new facet of the case to Reinhard Heydrich and requested permission to release Paul Thummel on his personal guarantee that Thummel would be kept under constant surveillance.

But Franta, if this were truly Franta, was too important to be treated lightly. Heydrich, in turn, presented the case in its new light to Berlin and requested permission to allow the release of Thummel on Abendschoen's terms.

During the early days of the Nazi Party, when it was a nationalist movement to regain the Reich's "place in the sun," young Thummel had been an ardent member of the inner circle. Himmler had been his close friend and had stayed overnight many times at the Thummel family quarters above the bakery, on which occasions the two young men, with equal fervor, planned glories for the Fatherland. Therefore Berlin too was half convinced and half eager to believe. Permission was granted, and Thummel was released on March 2.

To stall for time during which his "kidnapping" by the Czech underground could take place, Thummel told Abendschoen that he would set up a meeting with Major Moravek in a Prague alley on March 11. The exact hour and place were arranged, and the Gestapo planted a careful ambush. Thummel, in his Prague identity as Steinberg went through the motions of appearing at the meeting place, but Moravek was a no show.

Again suspicious of duplicity, Abendschoen tightened his surveillance of Thummel's movements. A Gestapo officer was to be with him at all times, even at night in his apartment, although only the top echelon knew of his Thummel identity. After the war one such officer, Patrolman Scharf, while on trial in the Peoples' Court in Prague gave the following account of his own tour of duty:

In the evening I came to his apartment. I had dinner with him and his wife and we talked until midnight. Then they went, to their bedroom. I was to sleep on the couch in the living room.

I slept so near the door that I would surely have heard if anyone left. But it was a quiet night. Only in the morning I found out that Steinberg had not been home. In the snow under the windows there were footsteps which I followed into the park, where I lost them.

Steinberg had met Moravek that night. I was not ordered to guard him any more.

Patrolman Scharf was replaced, however, by guards of sterner stuff. Abendschoen now demanded that Thummel arrange a meeting with Moravek in his own (Steinberg's) apartment.

Again a date was agreed upon, which would give Thummel time; March 20 was selected. The villa opposite the Steinberg home, the apartment itself, and the entire apartment building were filled with concealed Gestapo men. At the appointed hour Steinberg ambled forth, presumably to meet his quarry at the tram stop and bring him home.

He stood at the tram stop, waiting. The streetcar came and went, but no Moravek.

Steinberg returned to his apartment with a story about a signal from Moravek saying he would come the next day. But Abendschoen's patience was now exhausted. He arrested Thummel immediately and took him at once to Gestapo Headquarters to avoid any possible leak or warning to the Prague underground.

Nevertheless, some contact with Moravek had apparently been managed at the tram stop. Still working on the kidnap plan, Moravek met Bartos later that same afternoon to finalize plans for Thummel's hideout. The next morning—Saturday, March 21—he met Kubish and Gabchik in an apartment in Old Town, to detail their part in the rescue. During this meeting he again tried to dissuade them from assassinating Heydrich.

Now, he pointed out, with Franta's information cut off and the underground on the run, they would all be more useful if they could form a guerrilla unit. When Franta had been safely kidnapped, they could all retreat to the forest and fight on from there; many would join them. The paratroopers with their training would provide a strong core; perhaps they could convince England that the resistance would be more effective that way, and more paratroopers could be dropped to join them.

The Anthropoids were interested in this scheme, but they were as determined to carry out their own assignment as Moravek was to rescue Franta. They were eager to get on with it and had set the end of March as a deadline. After that they would gladly go along with the guerrilla plan. Meanwhile the kidnapping was first on the agenda, and they were ready to do their part in carrying that off. Moravek went over the plot with them and gave them their assignments.

At 7:15 that evening he went to meet another of his workers at a prearranged meeting place. Arriving a few minutes late, he found his man, "Dandy" Rehak, surrounded by Gestapo and fighting for his life. Although he could have slipped away unseen, Moravek pulled his own pistol and started shooting.

This drew the attention and the fire of the Gestapo. Determined to catch Moravek alive, they shot only to wound and cripple him. They hit him ten times in various parts of his body, including his legs. Moravek fired fifty rounds while trying to run away. Then, realizing that he was too badly wounded to escape, he sat down in the path of his approaching pursuers, held his pistol to his head, and shot himself.

The thwarted group of Gestapo, which included both Fleischer and Abendschoen, was furious at losing its chance to torture information out of him. In a frustrated frenzy, one of them emptied his pistol into Moravek's face. This stupid, vindictive act left them with no official means of identifying their prize quarry, except through the fact that the index finger was missing from Moravek's left hand.

Reinhard Heydrich reported his day's doings to Berlin by special delivery. Addressed to Secretary of the Party Martin Bormann at Hitler's Headquarters, his detailed description of Moravek's death indicates his recognition of the caliber of his adversary:

I am able above all to report that we were able to infiltrate into the Czech resistance movement and with that into the British-Czech intelligence service. After long interrogations of the arrested radio operator of the illegal transmitter, uncovered in October 1941, 41 more persons have been arrested and indicted with espionage (to a large extent this task has been performed because of the arrival of our army) ... The radio operator of this group declared on the spot during the first interrogation that he had sent the weather report to London and had asked for the dispatch of an aircraft with a new deciphering key. The very same night at 12:00 P.M. an English aircraft flew in and dropped a para- trooper with deciphering and courier material. The paratrooper was arrested a few days later. With further arrests which went through to January 1942, the total number of those arrested rose to 57 persons. Through investigation of the radio-operating material which was found on the spot and later deciphered, the existence of an important British-Czech agent "Franta" was determined. On the twenty-seventh of February it was found out that this person is the main agent of the Command of Counterespionage in Prague, Paul Thummel. Thummel is German baker, and is the owner of the honor badge of the NSDAP with a membership number 61574. He has been active in the intelligence service since the year 1928; i.e., at first he was an honorable agent of the intelligence service of the NSDAP, and since 1933 he has worked for military intelligence. After 1934 Thummel was main agent of the Counterespionage Command in Dresden. After the occupation in 1939 he was transferred to the Counterespionage Service in Prague. As far as one can evaluate the case of Thummel's high treason, we are of the opinion that Thummel was a very good, probably the best agent of the Czech intelligence service. He has received from the Czech intelligence service at least 40,000 marks. On March 21, 1942, SS officers from the German security police investigated known secret hideouts and post office boxes of the former Major Moravek, leader of the British-Czech espionage group and of the sabotage organization of the illegal Czech resistance movement when they did not succeed in approaching Moravek through a middleman.

After interrogating a number of persons who were arrested in these hideouts it was determined that on March 21, 1942, at about 7:00 P.M., one of Moravek's agents would go to one of the parks in the suburbs of Prague. Several Gesptapo officials occupied that park shortly before 7:00 P.M. in order to arrest Moravek's agent and so to be able to trace Moravek. The agent was arrested at about ten minutes past 7:00 P.M. after violent resistance, during which he attempted to use his pistol and to escape. At the first questioning of the arrested it was discovered that he was to meet with another agent at 11:00 P.M. of the same day because Moravek himself could not come at 7:00 P.M.

At about 7:15 P.M., when my agents started to take the arrested man away, Moravek unexpectedly appeared out of a side road, caught sight of his arrested agent, and started to shoot. The fire was answered immediately by my men. Moravek was hit in the thigh and calf and tried to crawl away. At 7:19 P.M., when Moravek was surrounded without hope of escape, he shot himself before my agents could prevent this. In this short time Moravek fired fifty rounds, without wounding anybody. He himself was hit ten times. When he was searched, two pistols of 9-mm. caliber and ten empty cartridges, coded material and radiotelegrams from London were found on him, which are now being deciphered. In the course of the liquidation of Moravek's group, so far *twenty-two persons have been arrested. We expect to arrest other persons and to penetrate the organization of paratroopers from Britain. Among the arrested are two former Czech military radio operators, who up to this time constructed short-wave transmitters for Moravek and were in communication with London; also three sleeping-car conductors, who during their trips abroad functioned most probably as couriers for the British-Czech intelligence service. During this action we confiscated: three transmitters, six receivers, many spare parts for the construction of transmitters, and a great number of radiotelegrams .*

> *Heil Hitler,*
> *Your Heydrich*
> *SS   Obergruppenffuhrer*
> *and General of the Police*

Paul Thummel was moved to solitary confinement in the prison at Kladno. His wife had been arrested too and was also taken there. Abendschoen personally undertook the interrogation and pursued his goal steadily for three weeks, during which he gave Thummel no rest. After that time Mrs. Thummel was released; but Thummel was transferred, still in solitary, to Pankrac Prison in Prague. It was hoped that he could still be forced to lead his captors to some of his former co-workers.

The capture of A-54 was a serious blow to the Czech government in exile, and through that body to the Allies, as it cut off their most direct pipeline to German Intelligence. But the death of Moravek was shattering to the homeland resistance. Although Bartos and Potuchek continued to maintain contact with London, they had bitter news to communicate.

Heydrich's continuing arrests reached out in ever-widening circles. His troubleshooting job in Prague was almost done. He would soon be ready to move on to other assignments.

Kubish and Gabchik were now ready to assassinate the entire Gestapo to avenge their friend; but Vanek, on whose shoulders the responsibility of leadership now settled, still felt that drastic action would bring further disaster. From the perspective of the London government, however, not only the planned Heydrich assassination but others too seemed desirable, and they hoped for more sabotage, more open shows of resistance. Accordingly on March 27 another group of paratroopers was dropped into Bohemia, each with his own assignment and with orders to make contact with the underground and to seek help from the Prague resistance workers in carrying out their tasks.

The leader of this group, Lieutenant Adolf Opalka, was an experienced soldier. He had fought against Hitler in the Czech Brigade in Poland during that country's brief but valiant struggle to repel its invaders. Opalka had been provided with the address in Prague of Mrs. Teresa Sojkova, whose husband had been one of those recently executed by the Gestapo. Mrs. Sojkova was left alone with a small child. Opalka managed to find his way to this hideout and later to make contact with Bartos.

Karel Curda, who jumped a few minutes later, was not immediately able to reach his contact. A farmer's son from southern Bohemia with a strong attachment to his mother, he was unable to resist the temptation to pay her a quick visit and assure himself of her welfare; after this risky side trip he returned to Pardubice, made contact, and waited in his assigned hideout for further orders from Prague.

Captain Oldrich Pechal had been entrusted with a supply of money for the Prague underground. He was spotted by two German soldiers right after his jump and captured immediately. However, he managed to escape by breaking his handcuffs and killing one of the Germans. He escaped from the other by losing himself in a thicket, where he remained throughout the night. Much later he managed to reach his assigned hideout in Brno.

Nineteen-year-old Corporal William Gerik, who jumped soon afterward, found himself in the middle of the hunt for the escaped Pechal. Forced to run deeper and deeper into the underbrush, he soon became lost in the unfamiliar countryside. He wandered, lost but in hiding, for many days without food or shelter.

Finally, chilled, starved, and exhausted beyond caution or care, he showed himself in one of the towns, told his story to a local barber, and asked for help.

This part of Bohemia, however, had been thoroughly frightened by the news from Prague. The barber turned him away, refusing even to allow him temporary shelter from the bitter cold lest he himself become incriminated. Desperate, Gerik drifted into a police station, hoping for the food and shelter which jail might provide. Instead he was handed to the Gestapo for immediate interrogation.

Although not all of the men in this group reached their destinations safely, the addition of these few was of great value to the underground. Adolf Opalka was from training days a good friend of Bartos's, and he became his right-hand man. Together they picked up the pieces which had slipped from Moravek's dead fingers.

In Prison

My companion, Weinblut, was allowed to stay with me for only a week. However, during that time I told him my whole life story, and he told me tales about his checkered career as a thief. During World War I he had regularly crossed the Russian border with cattle which he sold to the Germans; then he stole the cattle from the Germans, drove it back across the border, and sold it again to the Russians.

Among the belongings which he had brought with him, he had a piece of paper with a chessboard painted on it and a set of chessmen which he had formed out of bread. He was an avid chess player, and since I enjoyed the game too we spent much of our time playing.

Before he was removed from my cell, he told me that he went to prison school and that if I went too we could meet there and play chess.

"Just tell the guard that you want to go to school," he advised. When I was alone again, I asked the guard if I could attend this school. Promptly the next morning I was led to the classroom, which was like no classroom I had ever entered before.

The room contained the usual school benches; but instead of the students I was accustomed to, in each seat crouched a dark-haired, wiry, earnest Sicilian criminal, tongue clamped between his teeth in intense concentration, slowly and painfully copying letters as a Jesuit priest wrote them on a blackboard.

Most of the prisoners were illiterate, and they seized this opportunity to learn—either from scholarly ambition or as a break in the prison routine. They were hard-working, conscientious pupils. But on the last bench sat Weinblut, who waved to me. I joined him in the back of the room, and all morning, every morning, we played chess and chatted *sotto voce*. I have never appreciated school more.

Sunday was a gloomy day in prison. Our only break was mass. All the cell doors were opened halfway on a latch, and the service was held in the big hall. One of the prisoners played the violin. Somehow, during this service, I always wallowed in self-pity.

One day a prisoner killed himself by jumping from the third level of cells down into the big hall. He solved his own personal problems this way but left the rest of us extremely depressed.

Opposite the prison was a bawdy house which we could see from our exercise yard. A few times while I was in the yard, relatives of prisoners paid the prostitutes to show themselves naked in the windows or on the balcony. These were exciting times; everyone winked and waved and shouted and laughed and life was brightened for a few moments.

One day the guard came to my solitary cell and announced that I had a visitor. I was taken to the visitors' room, very puzzled. I knew no one in that country, and certainly I knew no one in that town.

On the visitors' side of the dividing screen stood a little man in a straw hat. He was a stranger to me, but I was glad to see anybody. Then he spoke to me in German.

"I am from the Jewish community," he told me. "We have heard that you are here, and we are going to visit you once a week. I have brought you some oranges."

It is hard to express how happy and protected this made me feel. From then on he spent half an hour chatting with me every week. He always brought a food treat—oranges, or figs, or something equally welcome which I rationed to myself and stretched out as long as possible.

Another weekly event was the visit of the prison barber. The cell was opened, a stool was placed in the opening, and the barber—himself a prisoner—shaved off my week's growth of beard. On one of these occasions he was very excited, very happy. He frightened me by dancing around while shaving me, shouting something in Italian. I could see that he was trying to give me some good news, but since I didn't know his language I wished that he would wait until his razor was put away.

After he left I puzzled over the words he had repeated, as I could remember them. "Ess scapato! La guerra finita! Mussolini finito! Ess scapato Ingliterra!" Months later, when I was out of prison and had caught up on the news, I realized that he had been telling me of the escape of Rudolf Hess to England with his own optimistic interpretation of what that escape would mean.

After nine months, when my sentence was completed, I was handcuffed and chained to eight other prisoners and transported with them to a prison camp in southern Italy.

The Paratroopers' Assignment

After her release Mrs. Thummel was permitted to visit her husband a few times, probably under hidden surveillance. During April she saw him twice in Pankrac Prison. Later in the same month she was summoned to meet him while he sat in a Gestapo car. This car, closely watched, was parked in front of the Golden Goose Hotel in Prague.

No explanation was given her for this odd trysting place, but she was told to enter the car and visit with her husband. She found him pale and thin but otherwise all right. Thummel told her that at the moment he was being starved by his captors so that he would be forced to confess, but he had not given in.

A spark of his old self appeared when he told her that the only respite he had had since his arrest had been achieved by his dictating all through one night to Abendschoen's secretary. The resulting manuscript was to be his complete confession. While the document was being typed, he had a good sleep; by the time it was presented for his signature he was quite refreshed and enjoyed confounding Abendschoen by telling him that it was all a pack of lies.

Shortly after this visit Thummel was transferred from Prague to the small fortress at Theresienstadt which housed political prisoners. The Gestapo continued to search feverishly for proof of his treason but could not produce any real evidence. Unwilling to publicize the fact that a German in high intelligence circles was suspected of treason, they booked this important prisoner as "Peter Toman, a Dutch national," and kept him in solitary confinement in the maximum security corridor of Theresienstadt. Only the commandant of Theresienstadt knew his real identity and the charges against him.

Theresienstadt also contained a larger fortress, under the same commandant, which was used as a concentration camp for Jews. As part of his intensified solution of the "Jewish Problem," Heydrich had made a sudden sweep of most of the Jewish residents of Old Town into Theresienstadt. The captives included Eva Fisher, Vlasta Chervinka's financée, and my mother. Vlasta, still dedicated to keeping an eye on his friends, had organized a more or less steady smuggling line into the fortress, through which he was able to provide food for distribution among the prisoners.

The Jewish prisoners in Theresienstadt were brutally starved— partly, no doubt, to hasten their deaths and thus the "Final Solution." Many resistance workers did what they could to help Vlasta's undertaking, but his main entree to the prison was through one of the German guards, whose cooperation he had succeeded in buying.

Atya Moravech, Rela Fafek, and their families were now deeply involved with Zelenka's quartermaster network. Their apartments were constantly in use as hideouts, and the Moravech home had become communications center for the paratroopers. Young Atya was actively helping with plans for the assassination of Heydrich; he also acted as courier between Bartos and the sabotage team. It became his duty to guide the paratroopers from one hideout to another when moves were necessary. It was his task, during the last week of April, to go to Pardubice to guide Karel Curda, the paratrooper waiting there, to a new hiding place. Bartos had received word from London that a bombing raid by British planes would take place over Pilsen; General Bartik had requested that the underground help the pilots to find their target. Therefore a hideout had been hurriedly found in Pilsen by Atya's mother, now known as "Auntie Moravech" throughout the movement.

Curda was guided to this place, and on the specified night he and three others (Valchik, Kubish, and Opalka) set fires in the area to serve as signals to the British planes. During that week six more paratroopers were dropped. All of these made successful contact with that group, then with others in Prague.

Of the new arrivals, two—Jan Hruby and Josef Bublik—had brought new radio equipment, which was always welcome. Another, Yaroslav Schwartz, had brought a new assassination assignment. This was not welcome. Professor Vanek, already doubtful of the wisdom of killing Heydrich, called one of his rare meetings in a hideout apartment to discuss the advisability of an assassination.

Schwartz's assigned target was Emanuel Moravec, a prominent Czech collaborator who had accepted the post of Minister of Education from the German invaders. After much discussion, Vanek and Bartos concluded that the killing of Moravec would bring down fewer reprisals on the Czech populace than that of Heydrich and would therefore be less risky. Both, however, felt that any assassination at all would be unwise. Accordingly they composed an urgent appeal to London, requesting that the orders be revoked. Using code names for the paratroopers, Vanek wrote:

From preparations made by Ota and Zdenek and from the place these preparations are made, we judge, despite their continuous silence on the matter, that they intend to kill Heydrich. His assassination would probably not help the Allies in any way and would have the most far-reaching consequences for our nation. Not only would it endanger our hostages and political prisoners, but it would also cost thousands of additional lives, and the nation would be exposed to unheard of terror. At the same time, the last vestiges of organization would be destroyed. Thus it would be impossible for us to do anything useful for the Allies in the future. We ask you, therefore, to give orders to call off the assassination via "Silver."

Delay is dangerous. Answer immediately.

Bartos radioed the message to London as soon as he could, adding the proper security introduction. At the end he added an impulsive comment of his own: "If for political reasons a gesture is needed, let it be a local traitor such as Emanuel Moravec" (Protectorate Minister of Propaganda) Vanek, to be doubly sure that his message reached President Benes—and that the London government appreciated its crucial importance—sent a copy by a young Swedish girl who was traveling to Stockholm. She delivered this copy to a Czech diplomat there, who sent it on to Benes in London.

After the message arrived, a meeting was held in London to discuss this urgent matter. The meeting took place on May 13. Two representatives of the political émigrés and two representatives of the émigré military intelligence hashed it out among themselves. The political representatives were inclined to respect the opinion of the homeland resistance, but both army representatives insisted that a "large action" was expected of the Czechs and that it was too late to retreat from the commitment.

On the recommendation of the majority present at this meeting, Eduard Benes, President of the Czech government in exile, answered Vanek requesting that the "large action" be carried out. He explained that the Czech Protectorate Government, by collaborating with the Germans, had created the impression of having effected a compromise peace with Germany, and that it was necessary that the Czech nation demonstrate its complete repudiation of the Nazi occupation. "In this situation," his message urged, "an aggressive action or revolt would be highly desirable and indispensable. In international politics this would mean salvation for the nation, even at the cost of large sacrifice."

Although the leaders of the underground had unanimously doubted the wisdom of the assassination, no such hesitation had even entered the heads of Josef Gabchik and Jan Kubish. As noted by Vanek, they had been making preparations since their arrival. Although they had been forced by circumstances to postpone the D-day several times, neither had for one moment intended to abandon his original purpose. They had studied Heydrich's routine; through his cook and his cleaning woman, both resistance workers, they had gleaned information on his personal habits. (It should be noted here that Czechs, including prisoners, were assigned to work for the Heydrich household. Once employed there, they were virtually slaves to Mrs. Heydrich, who did not hesitate to beat them or otherwise ill-treat them if they displeased her.)

A spot had been selected for the assassination. This was to be at a sharp bend in the street in Holesovice (a Prague suburb) along Heydrich's daily route between his villa in the country and his office in the Prague Hradcany Castle. It was his custom, in good weather, to make this journey in an open car.

The two young men spent hours loitering by this roadside, watching for Heydrich's approach and making calculations. When he appeared they would respectfully remove their caps and bow. After twelve days of such reconnaissance activities, they had pinned down the average hour of Heydrich's passage, the speed at which the car usually passed, the varying degree of police protection, the nearby terrain and escape routes. They determined what equipment they would need: this included two bicycles and two briefcases, which were supplied to them through the usual underground channels.

Gabchik had been specially trained to assemble a Sten gun very rapidly and with one hand. A Sten gun for the assassination had been provided in England and, disassembled, had been part of his gear when he jumped. In his Prague hideout he continued daily practice in the split-second assembly of this weapon and kept it always in top condition.

Kubish had jumped with a disassembled bomb, in the care and use of which he too had been thoroughly schooled. These two weapons would be concealed, on D-day, in the two briefcases.

Alternate plans were worked out for different eventualities with other members of their group. Since Heydrich sometimes traveled with police escort and sometimes not, the degree of such protection would be the variable which would determine the final course of action. Rela Fafek, who in addition to being an ardent worker had become Gabchick's girlfriend would give the crucial signal.

In a rented car she would drive ahead of Heydrich's Mercedes and make the turn in the road several moments before he did. If he were accompanied by police, she would wear a large summer hat. If not, she would be bareheaded—the hat would be tossed to the passenger seat of the car she drove.

Heydrich meanwhile was winding up his Prague affairs with an eye to his next assignment. Although the case against Thummel had not been proved, he was reasonably certain that the main intelligence leak from Prague had been plugged by that capture, and that the numerous arrests climaxed by the death of Moravek had effectively smashed the Prague resistance. For political-power reasons, however, he had one more task to complete before moving on to other urgent matters.

The German Military Intelligence (Abwehr), of which Paul Thummel had been a highly placed officer in good standing, must be made to grovel for allowing such defection to exist within its ranks. Accordingly Heydrich called a meeting in Prague to which Admiral Canaris, chief of the Abwehr, was invited. At this meeting a Gestapo representative delivered a lengthy harangue accusing the Abwehr of inefficiency and bungling, of giving its men insufficient training, and therefore of requiring greater cooperation from the Gestapo. A list of ten orders outlining what was needed was presented to Canaris for acceptance.

Canaris heatedly denied all of the criticisms against his organization and was unwilling to accept the Gestapo dicta, on the grounds that these commandments would have made his organization completely dependent on Heydrich. However, when the name Paul Thummel was subtly introduced into the conversation Canaris blanched, stopped talking, and bowed to Heydrich's terms. This meeting took place on May 18. Outwardly the Abwehr was still an independent organ of the High Command of the Wehrmacht; but actually, under the new orders, it would be forced to operate under Heydrich's personal thumb, wherever he might be stationed.

Heydrich's urgent business in Prague was now completed. He was eager to get on with his next assignment, which would be—he had already ascertained—the administration of occupied France, supervision of the Vichy government, and annihilation of the French underground which was gaining momentum and morale with the cooperation of the Free French forces under De Gaulle. His only remaining chore in Czechoslovakia was to proclaim "reforms" for the Protectorate Government, and he worked on this proclamation while completing his own plans for moving on to his next post.

Through resistance workers within the castle, Kubish and Gabchik heard rumors of Heydrich's imminent departure. This electrified them. They had been waiting for five months to complete their assignment and had no intention of letting their quarry escape, come what may. They now spent a reckless amount of time together, and with other conspirators, perfecting their plans and keeping track of Heydrich's movements. On May 23 an antique clock in Heydrich's office saw fit to give trouble. The usual repairman, a watchmaker named Josef Novotny, was called in to fix it. He bent with concentration over his work, taking care to replace each tiny screw with minute attention.

Despite his complete absorption, a document on Heydrich's desk caught his notice. This paper set forth Heydrich's complete personal schedule for May 27, hour by hour. Novotny was startled to observe that the day's activities included the Reichsprotector's permanent departure from Prague, by plane, on the afternoon of that day!

Seizing a moment when Heydrich had left the room, Novotny snatched this paper from the desk, crumpled it up, and threw it into the wastebasket before Heydrich returned. Then, satisfying himself that the clock and its chimes were performing in good order, he left.

Minutes later, a cleaning woman, Marie Rasnerova, entered the office and dutifully emptied the wastebasket for the Reichsprotector's convenience, without in the least disturbing him as he worked at his desk. The crumpled paper then speedily made its way through channels—to Vanek, to Zelenka, to Kubish and Gabchik.

Both Vanek and Zelenka were delighted to pass on this document which pinned down the day and hour of the hated Heydrich's departure. It is probable that they both hoped that the assassination could now be abandoned. However, Kubish and Gabchik interpreted the information quite differently. The morning of May 27 became their absolute deadline.

Gabchik's Sten gun would be the murder weapon. Kubish's bomb would be used as back-up, if necessary. Both would wear pistols concealed in shoulder holsters, to be used, if needed, for defense.

Both Gabchick and Kubish would be riding women's bicycles; but since bicycles were in short supply, this would not be incongruous. The battered briefcases they both would carry would also be too common to be noticed. One of the few privileges left to Czechs was the freedom to raise rabbits for food; a briefcase in which to carry grass for one's rabbits was frequently carried, even within city limits. In fact the briefcase found for Gabchik had been in use for this purpose until the day it reached his hands. The Sten gun would be carried disassembled; the bomb would be ready. At the Moravech apartment Kubish carefully went over its workings with Atya, to be sure that it was in order.

The morning of May 27 dawned bright and clear—a good sign, as Heydrich would undoubtedly ride in his open car to enjoy the beautiful sunshine. Kubish and Gabchik, in their separate hideouts, both arose with the birds, in cheery moods typical of young men on a bright spring day. Kubish, quartered in the Ogoun apartment, stopped to cheer Professor Ogoun's young son who was cramming for an exam.

"Don't worry, Lubos," he said. "You'll pass it easily, and tonight we'll celebrate together." Young Lubos, concerned with his own forthcoming ordeal, did not ask what Kubish expected to celebrate.

Opalka, staying with Mrs. Teresa Sojkova, also rose early that morning. He dressed carefully, inspecting the contents of his pockets, and took his pistol from its hiding place. He said goodbye as usual to Mrs. Sojkova and to Alenka, her little daughter, who knew him as Uncle Opalka.

"This will be a busy day," he said. "If I'm not back by eight o'clock tonight, I won't be home, so don't worry." Waving, he ran down the stairs and out to the street to catch his usual streetcar.

According to prearranged plan, the paratroopers went separately to a meeting place in the Vysocany sector of Prague, where they joined waiting members of the underground including Zelenka and Rela Fafek. Here each of the helpers was assigned a battle station. Rela was dispatched to get her car and her Easter bonnet and to wait for Heydrich at the outskirts of Prague. Valchik, equipped with a hand mirror, was posted at the bend in the road to signal the approach of the target by refracting the sun's rays. The others mingled with the street population to become passers-by along the route, ready to distract or engage the police if necessary.

Gabchik and Kubish rode on beyond the bend and parked their bicycles at the chosen spot. Gabchik removed his raincoat and slung it over his arm. Five months' worth of careful planning were about to reach their culmination.

If all went as planned, Gabchik would shoot both Heydrich and his driver with the Sten gun, then ride away; Kubish would snatch Heydrich's briefcase, doubtless full of strategic information of use to

London, and would substitute his own case which contained his bomb at the ready. Then he too would ride away. They would make their escapes independently and would lie low in separate hideouts until it seemed safe to make contact.

Each carrying his briefcase, the two ambled to their posts, a few feet apart, every motion premeditated. They assumed their accustomed pose of casual loiterers. Opalka slouched nonchalantly in a nearby doorway, ready to do what might be needed to cover their escape.

The spot beyond the bend had been selected because the road curved sharply at that point, forcing a driver to brake his car and to make the turn slowly. It was a blind turn in both directions. They waited for the prearranged signals to tell them what to expect.

At 10:31 Rela Fafek drove slowly around the corner in her rented car, bareheaded.

Gabchik smoothly assembled his Sten gun with one hand without removing it from the briefcase. Then, discarding the briefcase, he hid the gun under his coat.

Seconds later Valchik's signal came—the bright, restless flashes from the mirror. Gabchik now dropped his coat and stepped into the road. He aimed at the bend around which the open Mercedes soon appeared, taking the curve carefully. The target was perfect. The aim was perfect. He pulled the trigger.

He pulled it again. Nothing happened.

The gun was jammed. A shred of grass from the briefcase had canceled out all the planning.

Kubish, tense and ready, leaped into action. As both Heydrich and his chauffeur drew their pistols to shoot him down, Kubish reached into his briefcase, withdrew the bomb, and hurled it toward Heydrich, who was now standing up in the car aiming at the stunned Gabchik.

The bomb exploded near the car's rear wheel, shattering the door. Heydrich, wounded and immobilized, dropped his pistol. Fragments of exploding debris hit Kubish in the face, but despite impaired vision he managed to jump on his bicycle and pedal away, bleeding profusely.

Gabchik, starting to run, dropped his useless gun, drew his shoulder pistol, and shot the now pursuing chauffeur in both legs. Then he too escaped. Heydrich was still standing upright, probably in shock, waiting for help to come. But he found himself surrounded by stony-faced pedestrians who noticed nothing out of order.

One lone woman—a collaborator—recognizing Heydrich, turned in agitation to those around her, appealing for aid.

"It is Herr Heydrich!" she screamed. "Help him! Help him! It is the Reichsprotector!"

The unsympathetic passers-by made various sarcastic comments before they melted away. "The hospital is just around the corner," one suggested. "Let him walk!" A trolley lumbered around the bend; its driver and its passengers peered curiously but were not inclined to stop. Heydrich's lone sympathizer forced a truck to halt by blocking its path and demanded assistance from the driver.

The truck driver, noticing the SS uniform, apologized profusely and politely but explained that his truck was already too heavily loaded. He drove on.

Finally the woman succeeded in stopping a small station wagon; the driver of this car was willing to help the Reichsprotector. Heydrich tried to make the transfer from his own disabled car by himself, but he could not. When he tried to move, he collapsed. His two rescuers were forced to lift him, awkwardly and painfully, into the back of the car. They took him to the nearby hospital.

Kubish meanwhile pedaled furiously for a few blocks—past the hospital—to the nearest refuge that he knew of, the apartment of his friends the Novaks. Leaving his bicycle to slide to the ground in front of the building, he stumbled indoors.

Marie Novak washed his wounds and did what she could to stop the bleeding. She gave him clean clothes, her husband's railwayman's uniform, and disposed of the blood-soaked suit he had been wearing. While she was helping him, her fourteen-year-old daughter slipped outside and hid the bloodstained bicycle.

Disguised and burning to know how Gabchik had fared, Kubish followed Marie's urging and visited a resistance doctor who treated his badly wounded eye. Then, restless and anxious, he wandered the streets of Prague in search of a safe hiding place.

Gabchik was unhurt. He had escaped on foot to the Svatos home in the Old Town section, where he too changed clothes while listening to his own description blared from a street loudspeaker.

Heydrich was injured at about 10:33 on that morning. By eleven o'clock all Prague knew of the attack. Mrs. Sojkova at her job in a dentist's office was doing some filing when the broadcast broke the silence. She stiffened and thought immediately of Opalka. Was he involved? If so, dared she shelter him? She bent back to her work, trying to force her fingers to carry on through the rest of the day.

A Catholic Jew

The prison camp to which I was sent contained a mixture of political prisoners and prisoners of war. There were about two thousand of us—Yugoslavs, Czechs, Poles, Englishmen, and Frenchmen. We lived in barracks surrounded by barbed wire and guarded by Italian Blackshirts.

Compared with German concentration camps, this camp was a luxury hotel. The Italians treated prisoners as though they were indeed people like themselves. The only restrictions were the lack of freedom and the perpetual hunger. We never had enough food.

I became very friendly with a young Polish soldier who lived in my barracks. Zbigniew Jakubek was my own age, and since all Slavic languages resemble each other we were able to communicate. He had fought in the Polish army and was a prisoner of war.

The prisoners in this camp were allowed to work in the forest, cutting down acacia trees and making drainage ditches to prevent the spread of malaria in that part of the country. In the course of our work we came in contact with the local population. The people in that area were farmers who were very poor, and also very kind and helpful.

A lively exchange business started. We exchanged our shirts, old shoes, and any clothing we could scrape up in return for food: bread, rice, cheese, and olive oil.

During rest breaks, known in Italy as siestas, we sat around and chatted with the farmers. By this time I too could speak a little of the language. The farmers would always ask, of course, why we found ourselves in prison camp; once I explained that I had had to escape from my country because I was a Jew.

My listeners were interested but puzzled. "What is a Jew?" they asked.

"It's my religion," I said.

There was a nodding of heads in understanding. They knew about religion very well. But they wanted more specific information.

"Are you a Catholic Jew or a Protestant Jew?"

I said I was a Catholic Jew, which pleased them very much. They smiled and slapped my back. "Sei nostro!" they told me. "You are our man!"

Frequently the sergeant of the camp police ordered me to clean his office, so I was sometimes in there alone. During one of these moments I noticed a pile of travel-permit blanks on his desk. Quickly I took two of them and stamped them with his rubber stamp. Then I put them in my pocket and continued sweeping.

Back in the barracks I surreptitiously showed them to my friend Jakubek. After much consultation we decided to try to escape.

The geography of Italy made this a difficult undertaking. To the north lay the Alps that bordered Germany; to the east was occupied Yugoslavia; to the west was France. Our camp was in southern Italy, which is completely surrounded by the sea. Our only possible road to freedom lay all the way through the "boot" to the northwest corner, over the Alps to Switzerland. We decided to give it a try.

Among the prisoners of war was a Canadian Army chaplain, a Catholic priest. Jakubek, a devout Catholic, insisted on confiding in this man before we left, so we told him our plans.

He was very helpful to us. He often received, through Catholic sources, boxes of clothing to distribute to the prisoners; so he equipped us with civilian clothes. He also gave us Italian money, and two Italian Fascist Party badges.

Escaping from the prison camp itself was not difficult. We waited for a dark night, crawled under the barbed wire which was not electrified, then followed the road to the nearest railroad station were we jumped a freight train heading north.

The freight took us to Sihari, where we bought tickets for a passenger train headed for Turino. Our tickets and travel permits carried us almost to Florence and might have taken us farther, but just south of Florence we ran into a bombing raid by English airplanes. The train stopped, and all the passengers were shepherded into a nearby bomb shelter.

In the shelter we were safe from bombs, but now we were asked to produce our "personal documents." These were identity cards bearing photographs, and of course we had none. We made a big show of searching frantically through all of our pockets for these identity cards, but we fooled no one; it was obvious from our speech that we were not Italians.

We were handcuffed and taken to the nearest police station, where we were questioned. There was no use denying where we had come from, so we told our story and the name of the camp, leaving out the source of our clothing and money in order to protect the kind chaplain. We told the police we had stolen everything.

Then they made preparations which we did not at first realize were for our punishment. They brought buckets into the room. They poured vinegar into these buckets, knotted up some towels, and soaked the towels in the vinegar. They had us strip to the waist and face the wall with our hands up; then they proceeded to beat us with the vinegar-soaked, knotted towels. This is very painful because the vinegar stings when it enters the pores. I have had a permanent aversion to vinegar in any form ever since.

Then they shipped us to Palermo. We were tried by a military tribunal and sentenced to half a year at Prison Island. This was the island of Ustica, a rock in the sea, about fifty miles north of Palermo and west of the Lipari Islands.

Hunt and Reprisals

Needless to say, as soon as news of the attack reached Gestapo headquarters all Germany was galvanized into punitive action. Both Otto Geschke and the ambitious, arrogant K. H. Frank hurried to the scene of the crime. K. H. ordered all exits from Prague blocked, roadblocks set up, railway stations carefully combed. Then he got on the telephone and put in a call to Hitler. The conversation with his Führer is reported in his diary for that day:

Prague, May 27, 1942
At 12:30 I was called from the Führer's Headquarters and I talked to the Führer personally. I gave the Führer a report on the attack on SS Obergruppenführer Heydrich. My report contained basically the same facts enclosed in the first provisional report of the Gestapo dated May 27, but without details. The Führer asked right away if Obergruppenführer Heydrich had driven without escort, to which I answered in the affirmative. This was sharply condemned by the Führer. Then he asked about the condition of the Obergruppenfuhrer. I reported as I had been informed by Herr Dr. Dick after the first operation. The Führer then ordered the following:
1. Until the recovery of the Obergruppenführer I am to be in charge of the agenda of the Reichsprotector.
2. I am not allowed to drive without protective escort. (He asked if I had an armored car at my disposal; I answered in the negative. The Führer said that he would put such a car at my disposal.)
3. All possible searches should be initiated immediately.
4. A reward of one million Reichsmarks is to be offered for the arrest of the assassins.

5. *Whoever gives the assassins any help, or knows their whereabouts without reporting it, is to be shot with his whole family.*

6. *Ten thousand Czech suspects are to be taken into custody as a reprisal. Also those who have committed political crimes, or are already in prison, should be shot immediately. The Führer ordered me to keep him informed. When I asked if I should come to the Führer's Headquarters to discuss the political implications of this case, as soon as we had a complete picture of the case and its consequences, the Führer answered "Yes."*

Considerably set up by this conversation, and eager for a personal visit with the Führer, K. H. took only enough time to set Hitler's orders in motion before leaving for Germany. Before he boarded his plane at 5:00 P.M. that afternoon, he had issued the following proclamation:

1. On May 27, 1942, an assassination attempt against Reichsprotector SS Obergruppenführer Heydrich was performed in Prague. A reward of ten million crowns [one million Reichsmarks] is offered for the seizure of the assassins. Whoever shelters, helps, or has knowledge of the persons or their whereabouts and does not report this, will be shot with his whole family.

2. Martial law is proclaimed in greater Prague with the announcement of this report on the radio. The following provisions are ordered:

    a. All civilians are forbidden to leave their houses from 9:00 P.M. on May 27 to 6:00 A.M. on May 28.

    b. For the same time period all restaurants, movie houses, theaters, public places of amusement are closed and all public transport is stopped.

    c. Whoever appears in the street during this time period despite these orders will be shot if he does not stop at the first challenge.

d. Other provisions are reserved and will be announced in case of need over the radio.

> *[signed] Higher Leader of the SS and Police of the Reichsprotectorate in Bohemia and Moravia*
> *K. H. Frank*

Elated with power, K. H. Krank also telephoned a report to Heinrich Himmler, who communicated his approval and made some further suggestions:

> *Special train "Heinrich"*
> *No. 5745-May 27, 1942*
> *9:05 P.M.*
> *To: SS Gruppenführer Frank*
> *Prague*
> *Immediately into his hands;*
> *Confidential.*
> *1. I agree with the publication.*
> *2. Among the ordered ten thousand hostages arrest, above all, all Czech intelligentsia in opposition.*
> *3. Out of the main body of this Czech intelligentsia, shoot this very night one hundred of the most important. I shall call you tonight.*
>
> *[signed] H. Himmler*

Unfortunately for K. H., who assumed that he would now assume Heydrich's post, even while he was flying to receive his Führer's blessing he was being superseded. SS Obergruppenführer and Colonel-General of the Police Kurt Daluege arrived in Prague that very evening, sent by Hitler to hold the reins while Heydrich was laid up. Daluege brought his entire staff; simultaneously German police troops, dispatched from Dresden, Vienna, Breslau, and Berlin, marched toward Prague to back him up.

Daluege and his imported staff lost no time in setting their grindstone in motion. Early that same evening large, blood-red posters printed in German and Czech appeared all over Prague bearing the new proclamations. At five-minute intervals the street loudspeakers repeated the order that everyone must stay wherever he found himself between 9:00 P.M. and 6:00 A.M. or be shot. With all traffic and all movement thus brought to a full stop, a thorough house-to-house, building to building, room to room search was initiated.

A cloud of terror descended on Prague, indeed on all Bohemia and Moravia. Rows of trains stood in the railway stations; the waiting rooms were packed with people who were trapped there all night. Military and police patrols went through the silent streets of Prague, checking and searching, on the watch for violators of the curfew. German soldiers, Gestapo, and Hitler Youth tore into the homes of Czech people, searching from cellar to attic. The ten thousand hostages and suspects were rounded up, among them many resistance workers trapped helplessly in their hideouts.

Adolf Opalka was not late getting home to Teresa Sojkova's as he had mentioned he might be. He returned on the six o'clock streetcar as usual. He made no comment about his day's activities, but he was obviously depressed.

Mrs. Sojkova, who had wrestled all day with visions of little Alenka's being shot if he were found in her home, was nevertheless relieved that he was safe. She offered him dinner.

He looked at her gratefully but shook his head. "Mrs. Sojkova," he said, "I just can't eat tonight." Since all of Prague was suffering from a similar lack of appetite, there was no need for explanation. Mrs. Sojkova left him to his brooding and fed Alenka, who was still young enough to be hungry as usual.

She did not have to remind him what to do if the Gestapo came. Their plans had been well rehearsed. The gravest danger would be the innocent chatter of Alenka. That night Teresa lay in bed like a wound-up clock, clutching her little girl, waiting for the alarm to go off.

Late in the night the bell rang. Already wound up, Teresa started ticking through the prescribed motions. She woke Opalka, who was sound asleep on the sofa, and whispered, "They're here!"

Paratrooper-trained to awaken instantly, he leaped into action. Wordlessly they pulled the sofa from the wall. Behind it was an opening to a crawl space under the eaves of the sloping roof. He wedged himself into this; she thrust his belongings after him—his pistol, his tie. The ringing became insistent; there were kicks at the door.

"Coming!" she whined, trying to sound very sleepy. Silently she replaced the sofa and put a cushion on the very top, to look as though it had always been there. Then she opened the door.

"I was sleeping," she said. "I had to get my bathrobe."

The Germans entered cautiously at first, looking for armed men behind doors. Finding only a woman and child, they became the Master Race. They pried into everything, throwing the contents of closets and dressers all over the floor. Mrs. Sojkova guided them around with shaking knees, answering their questions. They looked at the sofa and under it—but not behind it. Alenka was awakened by the turmoil, of course, but to Mrs. Sojkova's relief she set up a frightened howling instead of chattering. She continued to make this welcome, uncontrollable noise until the soldiers left. At this point Teresa, her knees failing her at last, collapsed and joined her.

The next morning Opalka, restless and anxious, left to search for the others. "I must go to them," he told Teresa.

"Won't it make it more dangerous to be all in one place?" she asked. "Here the worst is over."

"I must go," he insisted.

Teresa gave him her dead husband's warm underwear to take with him—for the others too. She also gave him a raincoat which had been thoughtfully returned to her from Pankrac Prison after her husband was shot. She was sorry to see Opalka go. She and Alenka would miss him. She wished him luck.

Miraculously all of those directly involved in the attack on Heydrich got through that night safely. By next morning detailed descriptions of Kubish were also being broadcast, with the added information that he bore a wound "either on the left side of his face, or the left ear, or the left temple." That morning too the first of the new red posters bearing the names of those who had just been executed made its appearance. These posters became a daily event.

Jan Kubish had not returned to the Ogoun home on the twenty-seventh—very fortunately for all, as it had been thoroughly searched. On the evening of the twenty-eighth, however, he stumbled to their door, completely exhausted, his battered face and eye badly swollen.

He apologized for endangering them. "But I can't go on," he said. "You're my last hope."

The Ogouns, parents and children, did not hesitate. Taking time only to arrange a hiding place in case of another search, they welcomed him, fed him, and made him comfortable.

During the next few days a new proclamation was issued requiring all householders to register every guest with the Gestapo, even those who came unexpectedly and stayed only one night. Failure to do so was punishable by death for the whole family. Since the registrar's office at Gestapo Headquarters closed at midnight each night, and a late arrival was no excuse for not being registered, many families were trapped by this technicality and were immediately shot. The red posters never lacked a list of names.

Nevertheless, the particular fugitives who were being sought so intensely did not turn up. All of Prague seemed to be helping to hide them. Of the paratroopers who had come from England, the only one taken into custody at this time was Captain Oldrich Pechal, who had escaped from the Gestapo once and was still eluding them in the countryside near Brno. He was arrested again, but not before breaking more handcuffs and killing another German. The Gestapo managed to capture him alive, but only just alive. In their report they stated that due to the means necessary for arresting him "his questioning has been delayed."

Heydrich had not died. At first his wound did not seem very serious. But his appearance in the emergency room as the victim of a murderous attack by Czechs sent shock waves through the hospital which rendered nurses and attendants incoherent.

After the first superficial examination by the doctor on duty, during which Heydrich sat upright and grim-lipped on the operating table, observing every move, he refused to be touched by any but a German doctor.

Professor Dick, a German surgeon, was paged; he was located in the surgery and summoned to attend to the Reichsprotector. He arrived on the run, unbelieving as were all the others, but at the sight of Heydrich he clicked his heels, saluted, and bent respectfully to the serious business of examination.

Both Dr. Dick and Reinhard Heydrich were concerned with keeping the proceedings dignified. The various parts were inspected; all but the spine seemed unhurt. He was wheeled to the X-ray room.

The X-rays revealed that bomb fragments had penetrated Heydrich's ribs. One rib was broken. His chest was damaged, and fragments were embedded in the pleura—the membrane between the ribs and lungs. Another fragment of the bomb was embedded in his spleen (right under the rib basket) and would have to be removed immediately.

"Herr Protektor," said Dr. Dick, "we'll have to operate."

Heydrich refused. Understandably his confidence was shaken. He wanted a surgeon from Berlin.

"Your condition requires an immediate operation!" Dick insisted.

Heydrich thought this over. "Get Dr. Hollbaum from the German Clinic," he ordered finally.

Hollbaum was summoned. Heydrich was removed to the operating room with Dr. Dick glued to his side. K. H. Frank and the entire Protectorate Government assembled in the corridor, awaiting the outcome.

Hollbaum performed the operation, assisted by Dick. The wound was found to be eight inches long and to contain fragments and "dirt" from the bomb; it was serious but not expected to be fatal. For his convalescence, the patient was moved to Dr. Dick's second-floor headquarters, and the entire floor was converted to an SS arsenal. Patients were cleared from the ward, which became an SS dormitory. Machine guns were mounted on the hospital roof; the whole building was thick with guards.

All Czechs, except the necessary nurses and attendants, were excluded from the Heydrich premises. Reports on his progress were consistently optimistic; streams of black-uniformed visitors, bearing flowers, were permitted to come and go. It was a complete surprise to everyone, therefore, when suddenly, on June 4, he died.

Hospital gossip had noted an unusual quantity of morphine assigned to Heydrich's care. Jokes were made that his doctors were addicted. Whatever the explanation, on June 4 a sudden flurry of frenzied activity—a hurried convergence of transfusion equipment, surgeons, and black uniforms to the second floor—did not stem the tragedy. Heydrich died. The official announcement of the causes, written by Professors Hamperl and Weyrich of the German Pathological Institute, states: "Death set in as a consequence of damage to life-important parenchymatical organs through bacterias or poisons, entering with the explosive fragments, which settled partly in the pleura and in the surroundings of the spleen where they concentrated and multiplied."

Now the fugitives were not merely attackers—they were assassins. Since they had not been found, all of the Protectorate was guilty of sheltering them. All of the Protectorate was accessory to the crime, and all of the Protectorate must be punished.

On the fifth of June armored vehicles drove through the streets of Prague to remind Czechs of the strength and determination of the German occupiers. Mass executions, already a daily event, were now performed with no pretense, at trials. But the mass executions, the curfews, the searches, the reward (now twenty million crowns) produced no sign of the culprits. Therefore an example must be made, a lesson must be taught, to the entire Czech nation.

Hitler himself selected Lidice as the sacrifice. Lidice was a mining village about fifteen miles from Prague. Its inhabitants were accused of having sheltered paratroopers and were sentenced—without trial, proof, or warning—to execution. Lidice would be wiped from the map.

It has never been conspicuous on the map. It is hard to understand why this little town, among so many like it, drew Hitler's vindictive notice. Nestled on the side of a hill, it consisted of a few hundred small sandstone and stucco buildings with red tile roofs, and its only distinctions were a beautiful baroque church, a large school, and a Sokol gymnasium. At night, behind the hill, the glow from the blast furnaces of the steel mills where most Lidice men worked cast a permanent halo over the sleeping town. It was at night that the blow fell.

It takes planning and precision to destroy a town artificially, but the Germans planned well. The job was delegated by Hitler, through K. H. Frank, to Horst Bohme of the Gestapo. On the night of June 9, police and army units under Bohme's command surrounded the unsuspecting community. Groups of soldiers went from house to house and wakened the sleeping populace by knocking out all windows. Without explanation the women were ordered to collect food for three days. Then all—men, women, and children—were herded to the village square.

Here they were sorted: men here, women and children there. They stood, numbly watching and wondering, while the Germans collected radios, bicycles, sewing machines, farm machinery, farm animals from their houses and barns. Dogs, running around in bewilderment, were shot when they crossed a soldier's path, and left to lie where they fell.

After the valuables had been salvaged, women and children were herded into trucks and driven away—many to end in the gas chambers. All of this had been accomplished by daybreak. And then, at daybreak, the men were summarily shot. *All* of the men, and *all* boys over sixteen.

A detail of Jews was imported from Theresienstadt Fortress to dig a mass grave for the victims. When this had been done, and the town had been completely cleared of material considered useful by the Germans, the houses were set on fire. Walls which resisted fire were leveled by explosives. Then tractors and heavy farm equipment were brought in to plow under all vestiges of what had once been a village. The ground where Lidice had stood would be planted with grass.

On June 10, the same day as the event, the following announcement was made to the Czech people, on red posters:

Criminal Court in Bohemia: In the course of the search for the murders of SS Obergruppenführer Heydrich, unshakable proof was found that the inhabitants of Lidice near Kiadno had supported and helped a number of possible offenders. The respective proofs were found through investigation without the help of the local population. Their positive attitude toward the assassination is emphasized by further deeds, hostile to the Reich, as for example the circulation of antistate leaflets, the hiding of arms and ammunition, the possession of an illegal transmitter and rationed goods, and the fact that some inhabitants of Lidice are abroad in the service of the enemy. With respect to the fact that the inhabitants of this village violated the law in the worst possible manner, all adult men were shot, the women sent to a concentration camp, and the children taken away to receive a suitable education. The buildings were razed to the ground and the name of the village has been erased.

The Reichsprotector in Bohemia and Moravia.

Years later one of three Lidice children who survived the "suitable education" told his story. He was six years old at the time.

In the evening we had potato soup and Father told me to eat and not to fool around. He asked Mother what the news was, because all day long he worked in the foundry of Kladno. Then I went to bed. I had no dreams, not in the beginning anyhow. Then I had a nice dream of how we were playing in the village square, the older children were singing at school and we shouted and then the village drummer came and drummed for us to be quiet. Only that was not the drummer but Mother who woke me up and wept. And I was not on the village square but at home in my bed and strange people in uniforms ran around; only much later I learned that they were SS men and the drumming, that was how they knocked out our windows. We were to dress and go out. They told Mother to take all her valuables—then I did not know what the word meant—but Mother said that she did not have any, only her ring. And food for three days. Father was pale. He stood at the kitchen dresser and was forbidden to move. Then we all went to the village square; there were already many people and children, Ema, Dagmar, Eva Venda, and all the others. The strangers in uniform carried things out of the houses. Our dogs were running around us, but the SS men shot them with their pistols; our Vorech was shot too, he crawled up to us, one German kicked him, and I started to cry again. "That's nothing," my mother said and caressed my head. In front of the church, books and different beautiful things lay, which these people had thrown out of the windows. Father smiled at me, he came to kiss me and took me into his arms, then he said something to Mother. The SS man came and took him to the other men of Lidice. I remember how he waved to us. They took us to the local school and our mothers went with us. Some of the children were so small that they had to be carried by their mothers. It was sad in the school, everywhere you could hear weeping, children and mothers wept and so did I. Early in the morning, I don't know at what time, trucks came and all of us had to get into them. Father I did not see any more; they say that they all stayed at Horak's estate. The trucks brought us to Kladno into a high school. Never before had I been in Kladno, never before had I seen such a big city. The houses there were as high as our church and also the school building was large. They took us to the gymnasium. Later some people came to look at us there; Mother said they were Gestapo men. They asked us many questions, looked at our heads, eyes, and hair. They wrote everything down and left. Then some other people brought coffee and dry bread. For lunch we had soup and some potatoes.

That day was Wednesday and none of us knew that in the meantime they had shot, in Lidice, our fathers and grandfathers. We thought, and so did our mothers, that we would meet them again.

On Thursday nothing special happened, black coffee and potatoes at noon, sometimes somebody came and wanted to know something, but our mothers were already tired and so were we.

When at that time I asked my mother why we were there, she said she did not know. That the Germans were looking for some strangers, but that there were none. We boys knew every barn, every shrub around the brook and the mill, but we never saw anybody. Mother also said that this was an invention of the Germans and I said to myself, why did they invent this, how can they do this. One must not lie.

On Friday many people came into the gymnasium and they put us children on one side and the mothers on the other. They told us they would go somewhere by train and we would follow them in buses. Our mothers did not believe it and did not want to let us go; we firmly held fast to each other, and those gentlemen in black uniforms had much work to tear us apart.

But they succeeded, because there were many of them.

From that moment I never saw Mother again. I shouted to her, not to be afraid, that I would not fall off the truck, that I would hold myself, but then the SS men drew their pistols and began to shoot into the ceiling, to frighten us.

In the adjoining room they hung tags around our necks with a number and our name and we boys played courageous and said we would not cry, that we would show the girls how to behave. But then we cried too. They separated me and two other children from the rest and pushed us into a car. We did not know where they would take us. After an hour we came to a big town, many spires and houses, we went across a river and then they stopped. Prague, said one of the men.

So that is Prague!

We were taken to a hospital. Then we did not know yet that we were destined for Germanization. They did not speak Czech and we did not understand them at all.

I don't remember how many days we stayed in the hospital. But after a short time they shipped us far away, a whole day and a whole night, into some camp; maybe it was Lodz. There they put us into a large stable; none of us was dressed warmly and we shivered with cold. We could not wash and everywhere was dirt and we got lice. We were hungry; from time to time they brought us black coffee and bread. We slept on the naked ground and we did not know where our mothers were; they did not arrive and those people in uniforms had promised that they would come.

I did not stay long there. Several times they examined my light hair and then they transported me to Puskov into a children's camp; it was like an orphanage. I fell ill there and they put me into a hospital and never again did I see the rest of the children from our village. Only Vasek I saw in Puskov; he also had light hair.

When I returned from the hospital he was still there and said that they would give him to a family. We both were taken to Oberweisen and Vasek stayed there, I went on.

Some gentleman and lady from Dresden adopted me and always wanted me to call them Vaterchen and Mutterchen. Only I could not do it. I did not even want to, because I knew what my real father and mother looked like. But they spoke only German to me, they sent me to a German school—and I slowly forgot.

They called me Rolf; I wondered why, but they explained that this was my new name and to forget the old one. At school they named me after my new father. He was a driver, then he was drafted and after some time returned wounded. The new mother told me German fairy tales and I forgot how to speak Czech.

The war ended and I was still there. The word "Lidice" I did not remember.

Only in 1947 the Czech authorities traced me and so I returned home two years after the war.

And then I learned that the Nazis had killed eighty children of Lidice. Only a few of us survived. My good luck was my blue eyes and my blond hair. And I started to learn Czech again. I also learned that the SS men shot my father the very first day, together with the others. Nothing is left of our village but the plains and grass. It was sad when I went over the meadow. Up there our school used to be, and further ahead was the village square, and the church and our houses. All that has disappeared. My mother I met again. She recognized me by three scars which I had from childhood on my breast. And I, though I had forgotten how to speak Czech, remembered the color of our cow.

Horst Bohme's dutiful report of the destruction of Lidice was submitted to his superiors, Kurt Daluege and K. H. Frank, on June 12. The report (which follows) gives a vivid picture of the frame of mind in which the Germans approached their task, and of the dogged determination with which they overcame the few technical difficulties which they encountered while destroying a living town:

Prague, June 12, 1942

Secret—by messenger
re: Reprisals against the locality
of Lidice, district of Kladno

I. On June 9, 1942, at 7:45 P.M. I was informed over the telephone by SS Obergruppenführer Frank from Berlin that the Führer had decided that Lidice should be burned down. Adult men were to be shot, women put into the concentration camp, and the children were to get a suitable education. The fire department was to be employed. Thereupon the following has been done:
1. The locality was first surrounded by a police regiment.
2. This regiment was at night relieved by 200 men of the army from the 480th Regiment in Slany. The police arrested all inhabitants and concentrated them in the locality.
3. Women and children—that is, 198 women and 98 children—were taken by truck to a gymnasium in Kladno. A platoon of gendarmes guarded them there.
4. After the arrival of two further platoons of security police from Prague, cattle, grain, agricultural machinery, bicycles, sewing

machines, and other valuable consumer objects were collected and taken away. They are:

32 horses
167 head of cattle
150 pigs
144 goats
16 sheep
a not yet counted number of poultry and rabbits
a not yet counted amount of grain and fodder
32 farm carriages
3 electromotors
1 circular saw
1 plow
3 hand carriages
1 sewing machine
Transported to estate in Bustehrady

100 bicycles
3 motorcycles
1 car
3 pairs of scales
1 meat grinder
40 featherbeds
74 pillows
3 baby carriages
18 radio sets
27 sewing machines
1 electrical washing machine
96 men's boots
83 women's shoes

*a large amount of foodstuff and consumer goods
Transported to the Gestapo at Kladno*

The inventory was performed by protectorate gendarmes under the command of a citizen of German nationality, Colonel Vit.

5. At daybreak the arrested adult men were identified as 173 men, who immediately afterward were shot by a police platoon numbering 1/2/20 [1 officer, 2 NCO's, 20 policemen].

6. After the clearing out, Lidice was set on fire; the army put at our disposal 200 liters of gasoline. An additional necessary amount of 300 liters of kerosene were furnished by the Gestapo.

7. After detailed instructions were received from an officer of the fire police on how to set a fire, the first house was set on fire at 7:00 A.M. on June 10, 1942. At ten o'clock all houses in Lidice were on fire.

8. A group of Jews from the Theresienstadt Ghetto buried the corpses of the men who had been shot, in a mass grave in Lidice, on June 11, 1942.
9. On June 11, 1942, a platoon of SS Pioneers numbering 1/1/35 [1 officer, 1 NCO, 35 men] was employed to blow up the walls. This platoon was not sufficient, because according to the opinion of experts, two strong platoons, equipped with the best tools, would have to work at least fourteen days.

10. I was ordered to secure other objects of value, such as agricultural machines and iron suitable for scrapping. Three detachments of the Reich's Labor Service were employed, and they also served as a demolishing squad.

11. The land office in Prague was ordered to take over the entire area of Lidice for agricultural purposes.

12. The children will be removed on June 12 in the evening.

13. The arrested women will be transported to concentration camps on June 13. Because only the Czech fire department was at our disposal, it was not used.

II. Submitted to SS Obergruppenführer Daluege with the request that it be taken into consideration.

III. To SS Gruppenführer K. H. Frank.

On the Rock

Jakubek and I were imprisoned for over six months on the rock of Ustica, during which time we each lost about forty pounds. We might have been forgotten there, as many of the prisoners seemed to be, but through the intervention of the priest to whom Jakubek confessed we were sent back to the camp in southern Italy soon after our sentences had been completed.

We were glad to get back. The prison camp from which we had escaped, compared with Ustica, now seemed like home. We were welcomed back to our barracks with a festive meal which our fellow prisoners had scraped together, and which included real meat, something we had not even seen for six months. We devoured the meat in short order. After we had eaten it, we were told that it was dog meat.

When winter set in, however, we were hungry again and very cold. We could no longer work in the fields, therefore could not trade with the local farmers. Since our jackets and sweaters had all been traded for food during the warm weather, we just had blankets to wrap up in.

Every day, in that camp, a newspaper was delivered which the prisoners pored over. Of course we all followed the military and political events very closely. We were full of hope when Germany attacked Russia, because we felt that the Russians would beat the Nazis; when in 1941 the Americans joined in on the Allied side, we were convinced that the outcome was only a matter of time and, for us, a matter of surviving.

When we read of Heydrich's assassination one fine spring day, there was great secret rejoicing; we all hoped and believed that this act of Czech defiance would be a setback for Germany. Then, a few days later, we read of the destruction of Lidice and our joy died.

During this period of the war, both British and American planes frequently bombarded southern Italy. On one occasion American fighter planes strafed our prison with machine guns, probably mistaking it for an Italian military encampment. Many prisoners died, many were wounded; during that short attack we felt completely friendless—both sides were our enemy.

As the Allies drew closer, we both hoped for and feared their approach. The grapevine told us that the Germans were killing Jews in their Final Solution drive. Many of us expected to be sent north and exterminated.

At that time I received a letter from the International Red Cross of Switzerland. When the envelope reached me, it flashed through my head that only Vlasta could have managed to get a message for me into Switzerland; people from the film studio made frequent trips to neutral countries, and he would know which one to trust. I tore the letter open eagerly, hoping for news—but it was bad news. My mother had died in the Theresienstadt concentration camp.

Dazed, I drifted around the prison camp all day, trying to absorb the fact that I would never see my mother again. I tried to imagine how she had died, then tried not to imagine it. No details were included. I had no way of knowing whether her death had been "natural" (from illness or starvation) or whether it had been caused by some inhuman Nazi atrocity.

I have never been able to find out how my mother died. She was probably a helpless victim of Hitler's speeded-up attempt at a Final Solution.

The Final Resistance

I.

The destruction of Lidice left all of Czechoslovakia in a state of shock. However, despite this—despite the ruthlessness of the reprisals, the continuing arrests and the daily executions—the young assassins were not betrayed to the authorities as the Germans had expected. All of Prague seemed determined to protect the young men who had killed the tyrant.

Their selfless deed had made a public statement which expressed the deep resentment and defiance of enslaved Czechoslovakia. Czechoslovakia, although helpless in its chains, stood ready and eager to endorse that statement. The heart of Prague opened to receive them, to hide them deep within and to supply them with food, warm clothing, and ammunition for self-defense. The paratroopers themselves, several of them, now gathered in a common hiding place. They were aghast at the carnage which was being perpetrated. Kubish and Gabchik, especially, felt responsible for the mass tortures, mass murders of innocent people, and felt that they should stop the blood bath by giving themselves up.

By now, however, the remaining mainstays of the resistance—Vanek, Bartos, Zelenka, Marie Moravech—were convinced that the reprisals would have happened anyway. A copy of a situation report from Heydrich to Hitler, dated eleven days before the attack on Heydrich, had been picked up by a worker. This document informed Hitler that the Czechs were unruly, that acts of sabotage had increased, and that

Heydrich was waiting "for the proper moment to intervene like lightning and show in no uncertain terms that the German Reich is the monster."

Resistance leaders now believed, therefore, that if a violent incident had not occurred Heydrich himself would have invented one, as they had reason to know he had done many times before. All of their influence, ingenuity, and efforts were now directed toward helping the assassins to survive the hunt and to escape to safety.

Professor Zelenka had arranged what seemed to be a perfect hiding place, for a while at least. Although the Nazis had seemingly combed every nook and cranny of every Prague building, their examination of churches was only cursory. With the help of the priests and elders of the Karel Boromaeus Greek Orthodox Church in Old Town, seven men were secreted in the underground crypt of that church.

The quarters were by no means cozy. Cold, narrow niches in the stone wall, designed to hold coffins, served as bunks. With only one small window, close to the ceiling of the dank cellar, it was impossible to maintain a wood fire on the stone floor for very long; so the paratroopers depended on sweaters, blankets, coats, woolen socks, and heavy boots to keep from freezing. A supply line was established, with Rela Fafek, her sister, her mother, and Marie Moravech undertaking to collect clothing and food and to do the laundry; Atya Moravech acted as courier and delivery boy between the crypt and the sources of supply. Having managed to establish this hideout and provide for its maintenance, Zelenka found himself on the verge of both physical and mental collapse from the constant pressure of his three years of "quartermastering." Afraid that in his present nervous condition he might act rashly, and if arrested reveal secrets, he confessed his near-breakdown to his friend Vanek. "I can't go on," Zelenka admitted. "At least not for the time being."

Vanek accordingly took up the task of planning the next stage: getting the men out of Prague entirely. It was his belief that they could hide indefinitely in the mountains of Moravia.

A native of Moravia himself, he had a wide acquaintanceship among the partisan groups which had formed in these mountains. He was able to arrange with a forest gamekeeper for the use of his mountain cabin, and planned to evacuate the paratroopers as soon as possible to this new hideout.

The transfer would be made by carrying the men in coffins. They would be moved from the church to a funeral car and then be driven to the country outside of Prague, ostensibly to a cemetery but really to temporary shelter in the storeroom of a Kladno shopkeeper.

By June 13 all arrangements had been made, and Vanek visited the church hoping to see the fugitives and to explain the scheme to them. He asked the sexton to take him to Dr. Petrek, one of the priests whom he had known since childhood and who knew him well.

Dr. Petrek was willing to let him see Opalka, who was ranking officer of the group of paratroopers in the crypt and therefore in command. However, for the sake of caution, Petrek insisted that Vanek stand with his face to the wall. In this way he would avoid identifying the section of the underground catacombs from which Opalka emerged.

Vanek faced the wall obediently. In a short time he was invited to turn around. There sat Adolf Opalka in a chair in Petrek's office, wearing a heavy sweater and gloves in spite of the warm June sun.

"How are you all?" Vanek asked.

Opalka avoided meeting his eyes. He looked down at his heavy boots and said nothing.

"Where are the boys? I want to see them!"

"They won't see you," Opalka said slowly, still looking down. "They are ashamed, they are miserable!"

"But Heydrich died!" exclaimed Vanek, thinking that the jamming of the Sten gun and the only partial effectiveness of the bomb were the causes of the young men's unhappiness.

Opalka looked up now, his own eyes full of the horror and grief which his companions in the crypt shared. "The torturings," he said. "The executions. The innocent people. Lidice. I'm having trouble with them, Vanek. They want to give themselves up."

"Why?"

"They think that it would stop the murders."

"But that's nonsense! Did you forbid it?"

"Yes. But they are hard to control. They're very upset."

"The Nazis want the blood of thousands!" Vanek insisted. "Even if they sacrificed themselves, the killing would not stop. Besides I have arranged to get them to the mountains where they can join the partisans, instruct them in sabotage! They are trained soldiers. We need every one!" He described his plan. Opalka agreed to the arrangements and promised to convince the men that they could still be useful. A few days later, on June 16, he was able to report to Vanek that they were all eager to join the partisans and continue the fight. The date for the transfer was set for June 19.

Seven paratroopers were hiding in the crypt of the Karel Boromaeus Greek Orthodox Church. These were Jan Kubish and Josef Gabchik, Adolf Opalka, Josef Valchik, Jaroslav Schwartz, Jan Hruby, and Josef Bublik. Alfred Bartos and Jiri Potuchek, the radio team, were still in contact with London and were operating from a new hideout in Pardubice. William Gerik, the paratrooper who had given himself up in a state of exhaustion, had been interrogated steadily and ruthlessly by the Gestapo ever since that ill-advised day. However, since his problem was that he had not made contact with the resistance, no information of immediate importance had been wrested from him.

Karel Curda had been hiding out in the home of the Svatos family in Prague, where Gabchik also had been quartered. After the attack on Heydrich, when the house to house search was instituted, Curda fled from Prague to hide in his mother's home in southern Bohemia.

Like the men in the crypt, he was shocked and horrified by the blood bath resulting from the Nazi's hunt for the assassins. As the search permeated the countryside, he feared for the safety of his much loved mother. He may have believed the Nazi promises that the executions would stop if the culprits were found; he may have coveted the large reward. Whatever his motives, he decided to give what information he had to the Gestapo.

The events set in motion by Curda's treachery were described by a participant:

I was an officer of the Czech police in Prague, from which I was transferred to the Prague Gestapo into the office of Oskar Fleischer as translator and interpreter.

After the assassination of Heydrich, I was translating informers' letters, which from time to time arrived at the Gestapo. Mostly they were without signature, there were not many of them, and they had nothing to do with the assassination. Sometimes two neighbors quarreled, and one of them was a swine and informed the Gestapo that paratroopers were staying with the other and gave other untrue information.

One of these letters stuck in my memory. It was anonymous and said that paratroopers were staying with a certain teacher called Zelenka who taught in the Vrsovice sector. It is difficult to say who wrote it; I don't even remember the postmark. Each of these letters had its incoming number, therefore I could not liquidate any of them. At least I wanted to warn this Zelenka, but matters suddenly went very fast. Into the office walked a man whose name was Curda; he told so much that it seemed incredible. He had thick lips, a full face, and unsteady eyes.

They called me and I acted as interpreter several times for Curda. Once we remained alone in the room for a moment and so I asked, "Why did you do it?"

"I could not watch the murdering of innocent people," he said.

"Are you content now? Do you think the murdering will stop?"

He looked at me in surprise and did not answer. Then I was sorry that I had spoken with him at all; he was a coward, not interested in innocent people but in money. When I acted as translator for him again later, he looked at me in a strange way. I was scared that he would tell the commissioner that I had spoken to him ironically. Fleischer did not like me; he was after me and was even having me shadowed.

To come back to Curda, as far as I know during the interrogation he denounced all persons who had helped him somehow. Also the Moravech family in Prague-Zizkov. About the exact hideout of the paratroopers he did not know.

The name of Mrs. Moravech was enough for the Gestapo. Immediately a state of emergency was declared. Fleischer turned to me.

"You are coming with us," he said.

"I have work to do here, Mr. Commissioner."

"Don't talk nonsense. Get ready!"

It is difficult to remember the exact time; I only know that midnight was long past and day was already breaking. It might have been the seventeenth of June, Wednesday.

A number of cars went. We left inner Prague and made for the outskirts of the Zizkov sector. The commissioner made me think of a hunting dog on the scent. He trembled with excitement and told the driver to hurry up. I was ordered to remain at hand.

I had not had any breakfast then and had a funny feeling in my stomach. It was cold. Prague had not awakened yet. Tomorrow there would be new red posters on the walls with the names of the executed. We went under the railway bridge and turned to the right, uphill.

I closed my eyes and longed to be somewhere far away and not to know anything. If one could only whisper, "People, escape! Mrs. Moravech, you still have five minutes' time, we still have to go about four blocks; you have four minutes' time, wake up your son, let him save himself. At least he must escape, that is important!"

Two more blocks, then the street and the corner house.

We stopped.

"What is Curda doing now?" came to my mind. Fleischer raced to the door of the house and rang the bell. Wildly and impatiently. Then he looked around, touched the hip where his pistol was, and smiled in self-confidence. A long time passed, nobody came, he swore and rang again.

Finally, some woman came to open the door, maybe the superintendent. She wanted to say something, but Fleischer pushed her aside and hurried inside.

He stopped at the elevator. "Where do the Moravechs live?" he asked, and I had to translate. The superintendent trembled; maybe she was cold. She was scared and whispered something, then she pulled herself together and named the floor. All at once she shouted loudly, "Do you want to use the elevator?"

I thought, "She is speaking loudly to let the people upstairs know." But maybe it only seemed so to me. Fleischer luckily did not notice anything. I translated the sentence, he waved his hand and ran up the stairs. She shouted after him, asking if she should lock the house door, and he said, "Get away, woman, and mind your own business!"

Upstairs he looked at the names on the doors, finally found the right one and rang the bell. We waited and the house was quiet. Then we heard steps in the apartment and somebody opened the door. Fleischer did not wait but pushed inside and his men with him. I was told to stay in front of the door for the time being. What happened inside I don't know. After about five minutes they came for me. I went inside and saw three people standing with their faces to the wall: an elderly man, a woman, and a youngster. They were the Moravech family.

"Where are the paratroopers?" Fleischer shouted, and I translated. He was furious, because he had thought he was going to find the people who committed the assassination there. The Gestapo turned everything upside down. They were looking for the smallest trace but all in vain.

Mr. Moravech answered, "I don't know about any."

Fleischer shouted, "We'll make you remember!" Then he disappeared into the adjoining room.

"May I go to the bathroom?" Mrs. Moravech whispered. The Gestapo man who stood there said something rude.

"Please, sir, I really have to go!"

"You swine, don't make up stories!" the Gestapo man shouted and hit her across the face. Then he went after Fleischer. For a couple of seconds I stayed alone with them. Mrs. Moravech held on to the wall and turned to me.

"Go ahead, lady," I said, though I was not entitled to do so. She thanked me and went. At that moment Fleischer reappeared.

"Where is that woman?" he asked immediately.

"She had to go to the bathroom."

He looked at me furiously and said, "You idiot!" and hurried to the bathroom. He kicked the door open. Mrs. Moravech was still standing, with a strange smile on her face; then her face contorted and she slid slowly to the floor.

"Water!" Fleischer shouted. They brought water, put a wet towel on her, they did everything possible. She had poisoned herself.

You'll get yours!" Fleischer said to me. They carried her into the adjoining room. I interpreted a few sentences and the search of the apartment went on.

One thing was clear at first sight: the paratroopers were not living there. Mrs. Moravech could not speak any more, but there were still her husband and Atya. His eyes were full of horror and fear. Fleischer stepped near him, looked him over, and smiled.

They took them away, both in their pajamas. When Fleischer rang the bell, they had been asleep. I did not see them again.

Then we left. Fleischer ordered me not to leave my office. I was not called to the interrogation of Atya.

It was a horrible day and worse was to come. It must have been around noon when Gestapo Leader Pannwitz appeared in the doorway and ordered, "Let's go!" I took my coat and followed him. Outside stood a number of cars. I got into one of them and waited. In a moment we left. And again as we drove through Prague, people jumped aside and in their faces was hate. Fleischer was silent and the driver again headed for the Zizkov sector. Looking out my window I saw that we were on the same street as early in the morning. We stopped not far from the house in which the Moravechs had lived, but we went elsewhere—to a house on the other side of the street. The commissioners went confidently. They did not look around, they went up the staircase, and after them went the Gestapo men and then I as interpreter. Fleischer rang the doorbell. Silence. Then we heard shuffling, careful steps and somebody looked at us through the peephole. Pannwitz noticed that and ordered the Gestapo men to break down the door. All that happened in a moment.

But before they could break the door a lady opened it, and we saw a man flee down the hall and jump into the bathroom. Gestapo man Herschelmann drew his pistol and fired a shot. The others joined him. I jumped back to the staircase and noticed the nameplate on the door: Jan Zelenka, teacher. At that moment a voice called from the bathroom. I did not have to translate, the words were German; probably the teacher spoke it well: "Nicht schiessen! Ich komme heraus!" ("Don't shoot! I'm coming out!")

That seemed strange to the Gestapo, but Fleischer waved—in his hand he held his pistol ready—then the door to the bathroom opened and Mr.

Zelenka came out. He took two, three steps. Pannwitz started to arrest him, but at this moment Zelenka stiffened as if a hidden spring was in action, threw his arms apart, and fell down, before they could jump him. He had poisoned himself.

"Himmel Herrgott!" Fleischer shouted. But it was too late again. They took a carpet, rolled the corpse in it, and took him away somewhere, maybe to a doctor to have his stomach pumped, only the teacher was dead. On the way back they were in a very bad mood.

Despite the escape by death of Marie Moravech and Jan Zelenka, the Gestapo raid on their two apartments had yielded promising victims for interrogation. Oskar Fleischer immediately selected Atya as worthy of his personal attention. He retired to his office with Atya, a few stalwarts, and an interpreter.

Meanwhile his men continued to track down the names Curda had disclosed.

That very night (still the sixteenth of June) a detachment of Gestapo men raided the home of Hana and Vaclav Krupka in Pardubice. This was the hideout of Alfred Bartos of the radio team. It was also the place where he kept his files and intelligence records. Bartos and the Krupkas were miraculously away from home; but a thorough search of the apartment—which involved the smashing of doors, cupboards, and dressers—uncovered a bundle of documents of about fifty pages in a conspicuous red envelope.

This was Bartos's complete, current war diary, starting from the day of his parachute jump with his group, "Silver A." It contained military, political, and cultural intelligence and copies of messages sent to and from London. All of these were in code, but one deciphered text was found among them which provided the key. Also found were a supply of false personal documents, identity cards, workbooks, and police registry cards.

Names and addresses mentioned in Bartos's files convicted many Czechs of resistance work, some of having direct contact with the assassins. These names, plus those provided by Curda, plus the small amount of time it would take for the Gestapo to round up their bearers, spelled the end of the Prague resistance. Nevertheless, the information which the Gestapo sought so avidly—the present hideout of the assassins—had not yet been revealed.

Curda did not know it. William Gerik, who was "reinterrogated" from time to time, did not know it. Pechal, whose delayed questioning had started as soon as he regained consciousness, did not know it. The immediate and constant torture of each new person arrested had yielded no inkling. But Oskar Fleischer, in his office at Gestapo Headquarters, was still giving his personal attention to nineteen-year-old Atya Moravech.

Young Atya has become one of Czechoslovakia's (still growing) list of brave young heroes—despite the fact that he did ultimately break down. Many stories have grown around the special treatment he received from Fleischer, some probably apocryphal. One story has it that Fleischer taunted him with his dead mother's severed head. It is impossible to know the precise details of what went on during those private sessions; but it is known that Atya was, at the very least, brutally beaten. He was kept solitary but prevented from sleeping. He was starved, deprived of water, constantly harassed. It is also known that at one point he was confronted with Curda and told that Curda had already revealed everything.

Too much is known about Nazi methods, and about Atya's sensitive personality, for his countrymen to blame him for breaking down under more torture than he could bear. Only the poison capsule could have saved him from this, as it had saved his mother and Zelenka. But Atya put up a stiff resistance. This was proved by the length of time which elapsed before Fleischer made his gleeful exodus from his office with the name of the Karel Boromaeus Greek Orthodox Church.

Before taking action against the church, Fleischer mobilized an entire department of the Gestapo. Next he arrested, in their homes, the priest, Dr. Petrek, and the chairman of the congregation with his wife and daughters. He took time to torture these brutally but extracted no information.

In the meantime the "church department" of the Gestapo, some of them in plain clothes, surrounded the building and occupied the neighboring houses.

Vanek, driving up in the funeral car according to plan, found the square in front of the church full of men in uniform. "When I came to the Charles Square, I saw that the church was surrounded by SS men, and I realized with horror at that moment—all is over! All we had done and prepared in the last weeks was lost. I was ordered to turn back."

Four hundred Gestapo and SS men and officers had encircled the area. Machine-gun sentries were posted at strategic spots, and there was also a light cannon.

A shock troop of Gestapo and SS men started the attack by rushing the apartment of the sexton and forcing him to lead them into the church through a side entrance. When Oberhauser, led by the sexton, reached the altar, a pistol shot rang out suddenly. Oberhauser thought that the shot was fired by chance by one of his group and therefore did not pay any attention to it. In front of the altar, covered by a carpet, was a concrete slab which served as the entrance to the crypt. Upon his attempt to lift this slab a number of shots were fired from the choir loft. Subsequent events were described by the same Czech police officer who gave an account of Curda's treachery.

These shots were fired by Jaroslav Schwartz, Jan Kubish, and Adolf Opalka, who were on guard duty in the choir loft. Immediately after the shooting started inside the church, SS men started firing from the windows of neighboring buildings, especially from the school across the street. They fired through the church windows into the inside of the church, but of course the shock troops of the Gestapo and SS were inside. The danger arose that the Nazis might shoot each other, the more so because the Gestapo were in civilian clothes. The commander of the Prague Gestapo, Dr. Geschke, therefore ordered the firing from the neighboring buildings immediately stopped.

The Gestapo and SS who infiltrated the church through the sexton's apartment, were so stunned by the firing from outside that they left in disorder. Outside they regrouped, added hand grenades to their fighting outfit, and then entered the church again, assisted by another shock troop of the SS.

Now began the stubborn battle of the three Czechoslovak soldiers [in the choir loft] against the tremendous superiority of the armed SS, who attacked them with gunfire and grenades. The first to be heavily wounded was Jaroslav Schwartz, whose leg was completely smashed by a hand grenade. Despite his weakened condition through loss of blood, he repelled the attackers with pistol fire. Losing strength fast because of the profuse bleeding, he shot himself in order not to be captured alive by the enemy.

Jan Kubish was mortally wounded; grenade fragments all but tore him to pieces. Mortally wounded also was Adolf Opalka; as he collapsed with exhaustion, he swallowed a phial of poison and shot himself through the temple. By then it was seven o'clock. It had taken the Germans more than three hours to overcome three Czechoslovak soldiers.

The SS commander ordered his troops to use grenades. I heard the explosions as distinctly as if I had been standing inside the church.

All at once everything was quiet up there. A terrible silence reigned in the church. The SS men waited another moment before they ran up the stairs where they found the three paratroopers in their blood.

They dragged them downstairs. One was dead, the other two were dying. They quickly drove those two to the hospital to try to save them; the dead one they put on a rug in front of the church.

All at once they brought Curda and Atya Moravech from somewhere. They led them to the dead man and wanted them to say what his name was. Atya was dazed and weak; he shook his head. Curda was silent, maybe he was ashamed; only after some time he whispered, "Opalka!"

Now the Nazis were able to proceed without hindrance to the concrete slab covering the entrance to the crypt where the other four were hiding. They lifted it. Some SS men tried to go down into the crypt, but they were met with vehement firing. They had to come up again.

After that the Gestapo men led Dr. Petrek to the opening and forced him to call upon the paratroopers to give themselves up. But his words didn't give the Gestapo much pleasure. Petrek bent over the opening and started to speak: "By order of the German police I am to tell you to give up!" Thereupon they shouted from the crypt, "We are Czechs—we don't give up! Never! Never!"

And again a shower of shots. Petrek had to jump back and so did Pannwitz, the Gestapo man, who was all flushed and burning with eagerness. The SS men started to throw tear gas bombs into the tomb. But also without results. In the meantime the Nazis tried to break the boys' resistance from outside the church, where a ventilation slit opened out from the crypt into Ressl Street.

The fire department arrived. In a few minutes the Germans were pushing a searchlight through the ventilator opening. At the same moment it was shot to pieces from inside. Then they tried to push a fire hose into the opening, in the belief that they would flood the tomb and force the paratroopers to capitulate. But the boys shot the hose to pieces.

The Nazis then put a machine gun at the opening and started to fire. This must have forced the boys into the far corner of the crypt; there was no answering fire. The Nazis made use of this and again ordered the fire department to push the hose through and pump water inside. This time they did so without meeting resistance.

While water was flooding the tomb, inside the church the SS tried again to penetrate the crypt. The commanding officer asked for volunteers to let themselves down. Before they started this new attack, Karel Curda, the traitor, bent over the opening and shouted, "Give up, friends, you are fighting in vain!" Instead of getting an answer, a bullet whistled by his ear.

The situation for the besieged looked bad now; water flowed into the crypt through the hoses and those downstairs had nothing with which to push the hoses out of the ventilator opening. The slit was high and impossible to reach by hand. Simultaneously the SS attacked down the staircase from the altar.

The situation became hopeless.

The water rose and the attacks gained strength. . . . Those in front fell because they were hit and rolled downstairs, but Pannwitz sent in reinforcements. Then they threw grenades inside; they bumped down the stone stairs and their explosions were softened by the water into which they fell.

I, watching outside, asked myself, "How long will they continue to fire? Another five minutes? Half an hour?"

I don't know exactly when, it must have been around noon, but all at once from the bottom of the stairs four isolated shots rang out.

And then silence. Only the splashing of the water could be heard.

Pannwitz stiffened. For a while he looked in the direction of the opening in front of the altar; he waved an officer toward it. But the officer hesitated. He didn't want to go down there, and therefore he ordered two of his men to do so, and they very cautiously descended onto the first step, then the second and third, but the firing from the crypt did not start again. They looked at their commander and he indicated with his hand that they should continue. They had descended half the steps; nobody in the church or near it even breathed, the tension was so great; the SS men disappeared into the crypt, and then you could hear them calling.

The officer did not hesitate further; pistol in hand, he hurried downstairs. After some time he reappeared, wet to the knees, and shouted, "Fertig!" ("Finished!")

What else is there to tell? The firemen packed up their hoses and left. The commanders ordered the corpses of the paratroopers to be dragged upstairs to the church. Then they were carried to the street in front of the church—Gabchik, Valchik, Hruby, and Bublik—all good boys. Their faces were bloody, some were wet through; they had shot themselves and fallen into the water. There they lay, next to each other, with open, glazed eyes.

This is how the Nazis "defeated" them. They didn't get them alive, but they still had to identify them. With K. H. Frank in charge, they *brought people to look. They brought First Lieutenant Oldrich Pechal, a soldier, in a straitjacket. He had also been parachuted into Bohemia, but the Nazis had caught him when a gamekeeper gave him away to the Gestapo. He was barefoot and full of bruises. When asked the names of the dead he answered, "I don't know." The Gestapo beat him and kicked him until he fainted. When he regained consciousness he said proudly, "Yes, I know them, they are my friends and therefore I will not tell you their names! I will not give them away even if they are dead!" This was the answer of Pechal after he had been tortured.*

Then they took the dead boys away, they say to the pathological institute where they called many witnesses to determine their identity.

(Curda too was brought there again.) In the meantime, after everyone was gone, I slowly descended into the crypt. Through the little window which opened out onto the street, the one through which they had pumped water, some light fell, but only a little, and therefore I lit a match. The crypt was long and large, larger than I had imagined. I remained standing on the last steps because in the crypt there was maybe two feet of water. I was too tense to care about such details. Along both sides of the crypt were square black openings, into which formerly the coffins of dead monks had been placed. The niches, those farther away from the place where I was standing—that is, on the opposite side of the crypt, near the ventilator shaft through which the SS men had tried to enter—were empty. Instead of coffins, mattresses were in some of them.

I also saw a stove and a book.

The match went out and I had to strike a new one. And then another one. Some paper floated on the water; I bent over and saw that it was torn-up money. Maybe also documents. The steps on which I was standing were bloodstained, as were the openings nearest the staircase; maybe those defending the main entrance from the altar had lain there.

Water was everywhere. Muddy water, but not so much that the paratroopers would have had to shoot themselves because of it. The crypt is high and it would have taken at least the whole morning, maybe even the afternoon, to fill it so that the people inside would drown. No, I realized, the water did not defeat them. What then?

There is only one explanation: lack of ammunition. They ran out of it and saved the last four shots for themselves. They fought to the last cartridge. Under the little window that led into the street I saw a heap of bricks; they had tried to break through the wall and into the sewer. Their efforts were in vain; when they finally got through the wall they hit on clay, no sewer anywhere. And so they left it and knew from that moment on that they were definitely doomed to die.

I went upstairs and through the church out into the bright sunshine of the street. A German military band was just marching by and played a Nazi march. The music could not drown the grief I felt because the paratroopers were dead.

II.

There is no doubt that in contemporary German news releases the resistance from the crypt and choir loft of the Karel Boromaeus Church was highly magnified. The number of stubborn defenders was reported to the public as 127 paratroopers—a small army. But Otto Geschke's own report of the capture, dated June 25, 1942, kept secret until years later, acknowledges with a certain understandable embarrassment that only seven defenders were involved in that bloody church battle.

An excerpt from this lengthy confidential document underlines this fact:

... the catacombs and crypt of the Karel Boromaeus Church in Prague were finally established on June 17 and during the night of June 18 as the hiding place of the assassins and other paratrooper agents.

The Karel Boromaeus Church belongs to the Greek Orthodox Church, though by its development it should be called a Czech Orthodox Church.

On June 18 at 4:15 A.M. the Gestapo HQ in Prague took action against this church with the intention of searching its catacombs. About 350 armed SS men took part in the encirclement of neighboring blocks of houses. A few minutes after having entered the church nave, the Gestapo command from Prague was attacked by fire from the church choir loft. For some hours attempts were made to overpower the opponents and capture them alive. Three of them had barricaded themselves behind the large pillars of the choir loft and four were hidden in the church catacombs. Because these attempts were in vain or would have caused great losses, as the enemy even defended itself with bombs, this intention was dropped and the resistance was broken by SS shock troops with automatic weapons and hand grenades. Five agents were found dead, whereas two—among them one of the assassins (the one who tossed the bomb)—lived for a short while without regaining consciousness.

For a Czechoslovakian, the horror of these reprisals can never be fully recorded. Atya Moravech and Oldrich Pechal were both summarily shot a few days after the church battle. Colonel Masin, Major Moravek's former teammate, who had been captured many months before and questioned steadily, was also shot soon afterward—on June 30, 1942, in a mass execution of important members of the resistance. One hundred and fifteen people were shot that day, including a former prime minister, General Elias.

Despite the long and intense interrogations which Colonel Masin had undergone, he was able to shout defiantly before he died, "Long live the Czechoslovak Republic!" This was reported by a Gestapo witness.

A distant relative of Valchik's, who was rounded up in a mass arrest, lived (by virtue of a different surname) to tell an inside story of the nightmare:

Hell cannot be worse. We shivered with cold and hunger as we stood in the courtyard of the Theresienstadt Little Fortress, beaten, full of lice, in rags. It was after the evening roll call, but the order was that we should stay where we were.

We guessed that something was up. But what? A transport? Executions? Some hung their heads, others came up with different reasons to explain why they did not allow us to go to our cells and made us stand there.

Then two SS men came out of the building, bringing with them a table and some papers. One of them sat down on a chair, drew the papers to him, and started to call out names. Each person whose name was called had to run to the table as fast as possible, announce in German the place and date of his birth, and then proceed to the adjoining courtyard. There people had to stand in rows of five. Other SS men came with sticks to help those prisoners who were not fast enough. They formed a double row through which we had to run.

My name was among those called.

We soon realized that those prisoners who had some connection with the so-called paratroopers were being called. . . . I got into this group by chance. I had been arrested for underground activity. Along with me about twenty Jews and thirty young Ukrainians were placed in the paratrooper contingent. They had been slave laborers in Germany, had tried to escape, and had been caught on the territory of Bohemia. In the paratrooper group were the entire Vaichik and Kubish families, fathers and sons; in the other courtyard were the women and girls. Valchik, Kubish, Valchik, Kubish—everyone in the Protectorate of Bohemia and Moravia with that name had been arrested. Sometimes they were very distant relatives, sometimes they did not even know the men, but no matter what, there they stood awaiting their fate.

Only Gabchik's family survived because they lived in Slovakia, a Fascist puppet state since 1939, which did not fall under German jurisdiction. His father and relatives lived to see the liberation in 1945.

Besides these relatives, or more precisely besides those who had names identical with those of the assassins, anyone suspected of having actively helped the paratroopers were added to our ranks by the SS men.

Then one SS man announced that the next day we would not go to work but remain in the camp. Now we were allowed to return to our cells. You can imagine that we did not sleep. Everybody had something different to say. Somebody said there would be a mock trial for us, others thought of death.

I did not sleep a wink that night.

Those who were not in our group tried to comfort us with the thought that maybe we were going to be released, go home. Some people believed, them; the thought was too alluring. Others shook their heads; they knew the Nazis.

"You'll see, they'll transport us to a light labor camp," my neighbor said at breakfast. Another man, convinced that we were going to court, reminded us that at least it would be warm there.

And so we waited and knew something was going to happen. . . We could not defend ourselves, and we did not know whether to be afraid or glad. Then the others went to work and we stayed behind. We were no longer in any mood to talk.

Finally there came an order: To the barber in groups.

Did that mean there was hope?

Why would they cut our hair if we were going to our deaths?

Hand in all equipment: spoon, blanket, plate. Return prison uniform.

Now we were happy. They gave us our civilian clothes. Our clothes, in which we had been arrested. "Why our clothes?" one of the Kubish family shouted. "To go home in, of course!" and he started to embrace the others. "I am completely innocent, I worked in my fields and nothing else!" He looked from one to another and then was silent.

To the shower!

That looked like release!

But why did they beat us? Only just back from the showers and they nearly broke your back.

"Let them help themselves; anyhow it's for the last time," a young boy said; he was one of the Valchiks. "On Sunday there's a dance in our village. . ."

In the afternoon, at four o'clock, we marched to the other courtyard, where there were two cells for about twenty-five prisoners each.

Then they locked us up.

There we stood, tightly pressed one against another. Some of us still had hope. Others swore. In the corner they recited the Lord's Prayer aloud.

"Don't be fools!" a gray-haired man shouted from the window. "They'll let us go home!"

It got dark. We were hungry, and the cold touched us to the bone. It was raining again outside.

Late in the evening the door opened and an SS man entered, a stick in his hand. Behind him came two cooks with a kettle of black coffee. It was like hot black water and I hadn't had anything warm the whole day. And so I drank it. Then we remained standing; somebody tried to sit down in this press to rest a little, but that was difficult. The night stretched on and the raindrops fell.

The air was thick, oxygen was lacking, it was difficult to breathe. Some people had a fever.

In the morning SS men tore into both cells. It was still dark and again we had to go into the courtyard and stand in rows of five.

They began to count us, shout at us, and beat us.

Then the Theresienstadt commander, Joeckel, came and ordered each of us to hand in all our clothes except shirt, trousers, and boots. Some of us had put on everything we had in order to keep warm.

The SS men beat us with sticks and the first of our people fell. Next to us was a pile of clothing which the guards had torn from our bodies. The cold wind got to our skin and we squinted at the pile of coats and sweaters.

At about seven o'clock they brought in a group of women; they were crying.

At half-past seven they brought food; each of us got a small piece of bread and a little bit of margarine.

"The day's ration," said the cook and grinned.

Then we started off. There were three hundred of us. Around us SS guards, every thirty feet, with rifles. They wanted us to hurry, but we could not. At the front walked the women. It started to snow.

When we came to the station, we saw that the engine stood in the direction of Prague.

"We are going to court" was the word that spread through the column. And everybody lifted his head to look at that ordinary railway engine as if it were magic. The SS men ordered the windows to be kept closed for the duration of the trip. No talking, not even whispering. To the bathroom only under SS escort. No moving around.

We got onto the train and off it went. Some were looking forward to seeing Prague, others just looked at the floor. The SS were talking in the corner, three for each carriage. The regular sound of the wheels on the rails made you want to fall asleep; the uncertainty did not allow it.

My neighbor whispered to me that there were two possibilities: either to a trial in Prague or a concentration camp. If we went from Prague in the direction of Kolin, that would mean Poland and Auschwitz. If we went toward Benesov, that spelled Mauthausen.

Which was better, Kolin or Benesov?

Then came Prague. The loudspeaker blared something, as usual first in German and then in Czech, people hurried across the platform, and we heard the Czech language but were not allowed to move.

The first, the second, the tenth minute passed and by then it was sure that we would stay on the train. The notion of a trial disappeared and the only thought that remained was: Kolin or Benesov?

Benesov! Direction south. At eight in the evening we passed through Budweis and switched onto the rails to Linz. So it was Mauthausen for sure, the death camp. Now even the biggest optimists were silent.

"Let us sing at least!" somebody suggests. The guard shouts him down. Evening comes, our bodies and brains are weakened.

"We are already in Austria," somebody opposite me remarks, but nobody answers him

Suddenly the train stops. "Alles heraus, los, los zu Fun fen!" ("Everybody out. Into rows of five.") We do not see one another, we stumble around, it is pouring and in a moment we are wet to the skin.

New guards arrive, obviously from the camp. They are carrying tommy guns. Finally we start. They kick us, shouting, "Los, los, schneller." ("Faster, faster.") The streets of the little town are narrow; in a little while we get out into the country, which we feel more than actually see. The path beads somewhere up, we march through a deserted alley with bare branches, and instead of raining it starts snowing again and there is a strong wind.

They make us go faster. It is three miles to the top of the hill, I don't know, I walk counting my steps, then the trees; for a while I close my eyes, always walking ahead, the road is without end and on top is the camp. Granite walls appear out of the darkness. They lead far, far back; you cannot see where they end. Then we stand before the gate. Searchlights illuminate the courtyard. It looks like a stage set.

All those Kubishes, Valchiks, Moravechs, and the others are still with us, but another moment and we are separated; our group stands apart.

The snowflakes fall on our shaven heads. It is cold and we are not allowed to move. Orders and the reading of names.

We go across a stone staircase into a basement, where the bathrooms are situated. SS men stand there and beat us, ever more wildly. The first of our people die. We must undress and then go upstairs again into the courtyard, which by now is snowed in.

They are just leading away the paratrooper group, about two hundred and fifty bruised people with shaven heads. They chase them somewhere away from us; for a moment we can still see them, then they are lost from sight—forever.

The next afternoon the tall chimney over the adjacent stone building is belching dense smoke and at times we can also see flames. That building is the crematorium. And it was snowing all the time and the wind played with the smoke, slowly rising to the sky, which was low, sad, and dirty.

Karel Curda, the informer, received only half of the promised reward of ten million crowns for information leading to the bloodbath. The money was deposited for him in the German Bank in Prague, to be drawn at the rate of 30,000 crowns per month. (Later, unable to enjoy his wealth among his compatriots, he married a German girl and lived as a collaborator as long as the occupation lasted. After the liberation he was tried by a Czech court and hanged for treason.)

Alfred Bartos's captured files had provided the Gestapo with much information and several leads; but Bartos himself, his radio operator, Jiri Potuchek, and their transmitter were not immediately apprehended. Geschke gleefully reported on some information found in Bartos's files:

. . . the final proofs that we are dealing with orders from London are the radiotelegraphic cables, found at the place of Major Bartos, the commander of the group of paratrooper agents in the Protectorate, exchanged between him (from Pardubice, Bohemia) and London, which, I enclose. Incidentally, one of the radiotelegraphic dispatches, which he sent to London at the beginning of May 1942, justifies our nearly complete destruction of the resistance organizations in the Protectorate, for it is the assassination order given to Ota and Zdenek (cover names of the assassins) and suggests that the target of assassination be the Protectorate Minister of Propaganda Emanuel Moravec. The assassination order was not rescinded, but the appreciation of Benes for the paratrooper agents is expressed in the radiotelegraphic dispatch of June 3, 1942, from London. From all these facts it clearly follows: The idea, orders, auxiliary means, performance, thanks and appreciation for the assassination of SS Obergruppenfuhrer Heydrich were "made in England."

The Gestapo Branch Office in Pardubice, meanwhile, was bending all its efforts toward the capture of Bartos, who still sent sporadic messages to London. Having learned that he had an errand at the Krupka apartment in Pardubice, they arrested the Krupkas and lay in ambush in and around the premises.

At seven o'clock on June 21 someone rang the doorbell, two short and one long. Two SS men with drawn pistols opened the door but found no one there. On the opposite side of the street they saw a man whom they recognized as Bartos and immediately pursued him.

Bartos, seeing them and recognizing trouble, mingled with pedestrians to evade them and made his way rapidly from the scene. Snatching bicycles from passers-by, the SS men followed and soon gained on the now running Bartos. Realizing that he could not out-distance them, he turned and fired. Several shots were exchanged before he was hit in a spot which caused him to collapse. Trapped, he shot himself in the head.

With the usual Gestapo concern for the welfare of a prisoner, he was rushed to a hospital for treatment but died without regaining consciousness. Now only Potuchéck, with one lone transmitter, was still at large.

The Pardubice office now learned that the radio team had been operating from the nearby small village of Lezhaky. They reported this to K. H. Frank, who promptly ordered the Lidice treatment for the tiny village. The following notice appeared in the press on June 25:

On June 24 the village of Lezhaky near Louky (district of Chrudim) was leveled to the ground. The adult inhabitants have been shot, according to martial law.

The inhabitants had given refuge to Czech paratrooper agents who played a leading part in the preparations for the assassination of SS Obergruppenfuhrer Heydrich and had tried to save them from police interception. A member of the Protectorate Gendarmerie Corps stationed in the village, who was guilty of giving assistance, committed suicide before he could be arrested..

But radio operator Potuchek had not been trapped in Lezhaky. On the June 26 he sent the following, message to London:

The village of Lezhaky, where I was with my transmitter, has been leveled to the ground. People who helped us have been arrested. Only with their help could I have saved the radio equipment and myself. Fred [Bartos] was not in Lezhaky that day. I do not know where he is and he does not know my present whereabouts. I hope that I shall be able to renew contact with him. I am all by myself now. In case I don't find Fred, give name and address of his successor. Next transmission at 23 hours on June 28.

But there were no more transmissions. Shortly afterward, in a shoot-out with Gestapo men, Potuchek lost his radio equipment. On July 2 he returned to Pardubice, still looking for Bartos. On this occasion the Gestapo found him, cornered him, and shot him dead.

This marked the end of organized resistance in Bohemia.

Soon after the fighting in the Karel Boromaeus Church was over, the Nazis prepared a trial for the priests of the Orthodox Church who had given refuge to the paratroopers. The whole procedure was a farce staged by the Prague Gestapo, but it was a delicate matter for the Nazis, as the Orthodox Church was the official church of Germany's allies, the monarchies of Rumania and Bulgaria. The session was therefore declared public, although in fact it took place in Gestapo Headquarters and was presided over by Otto Geschke himself.

The trial took place on September 3. All of the accused were found guilty and were sentenced to be shot within the next few days. Then the

Nazis unleashed their terror against the whole Orthodox Church in the Czech lands. In order not to antagonize their allies, they specified that only the Orthodox Church of Serbian jurisdiction was involved. This church, throughout Czechoslovakia, was dissolved and its property confiscated.

The final roundup, imprisonments, and executions of the period which Czechs call "the Heydrichiade" took place at this time.

Rela Fafek, her sister, her mother, and, the little girl who hid the bicycle all died in a mass execution.

Otto Geschke's report describes their courageous last moments:

The majority of those who helped the assassins displayed a pronounced Czech, chauvinistic, and anti-German attitude. It is most conspicuous with the women and is a consequence of their former political opinions.

All of the arrested belong to the most antagonistic Czech circles. One can frequently hear them say: "We are proud to be able to die for our nation in such a way!"

Professor Vanek, one of the few survivors, tells of those days:

Day after day the Gestapo penetrated deeper and deeper into our network. After the Moravech family and Zelenka, they arrested many people in Prague. More and more people were lost.

If Curda was of the opinion that the executions would stop if he informed the Gestapo, he was at least very naïve. Just the opposite; now the Gestapo really got down to work. They tortured and pressured those arrested with the most brutal methods to give away other Czechs. Blood flowed, much blood. Nobody was sure of his life. In the morning, at noon, in the evening long lists of names were read over the radio. "For agreeing with the assassination . . . For helping unregistered persons."

What I had feared so much—and that is also why I asked London to call off the assassination—came true.

In the end they got me too. That was even after martial law had been called off in the Garden City sector of Prague. I was staying there with the Alesh family. The Gestapo came with dogs, and I nearly got away too.

I had not lived there for quite some time, but on just that day I went there at Mrs. Alesh's request to receive my pension in place of her husband and using his name. I sent somebody else to the Aleshes' for security purposes; this person did not know about anything. The Gestapo was in the apartment by the time he arrived; they knew that I had lived there, and they forced the man I sent to tell them who had sent him and where I was.

I was waiting at the nearby sports stadium. When they took me to the Petschek Palace, to Gestapo Headquarters, I remembered that I had a little tube of poison in a small pocket of my trousers. Though they had searched me thoroughly, they happened to miss that little pocket. In the little tube was heroin. That is an alkaloid which causes paralysis of the breathing center.

I thought everything over and saw no other solution. I was in bad shape; they had beaten me in the abdomen and so I made use of it and began to writhe in the car. I bent forward (I was handcuffed) and fished with my fingers in that little pocket. It went slowly and I had to be careful not to arouse their attention. When I got out of the car in front of the Petschek Palace, I bent forward again as if in pain and put the tube into my mouth, bit on it, and swallowed.

I was quiet then, though I felt blood running down my face.

"What's the matter, can't you pull yourself together?" the commissioner said as we stepped onto the pavement and crossed the street to the Gestapo building. He looked at the blood on my face and thought that it was from the beating and that I hadn't wiped it off on *purpose. But I had cut my mouth when I bit on the tube. They undressed me completely and again I had to stand facing a wall; they were looking for poison and did not realize that I had already swallowed some. When they turned me around so that I faced the room, Dr. Petrek, the priest from the Karel Boromaeus Church, stood before me. I remembered our last meeting in the church: all was in order then, and he went to get Opalka with whom I wanted to talk about the future fate of the paratroopers.*

They had brought him in to identify me. He went pale and bent his head. That day he was to be executed. . . . I knew him well. We had been good friends long before the Heydrich assassination; we were born on the same day, June 19, and his father had been my teacher in the first grade of elementary school in 1912 in Modolany.

He did not say a word. We never saw each other again. They then pushed me into a cell, where I began to vomit. The poison had taken effect, I was feeling sick, and therefore they decided to pump out my stomach.

I do not want to go into details. In the end I was sentenced to death. Because I was important for them as one of the resistance leaders and the one who had asked London to call off the assassination, they did not execute me immediately. "He can't run away anyhow," they thought, "and when the war, which we will win, is over he can clarify many things concerning the assassination."

I survived and today there is an emptiness around me. My friends, those who worked with me, are all dead. Or nearly all of them. My hair is gray, once again I teach chemistry and walk between the school benches. The Heydrich assassination has become history. For us, who by chance escaped with our lives, that time is the most terrible chapter of our lives.

Sometimes in the evening I close my eyes and remember. I think of all of them, of Kubish, Gabchik, the other boys, "Auntie" Moravech,

Zelenka. . . . Hundreds of others I don't even know by name, only that they were sent from Theresienstadt to Mauthausen to their deaths. Like cattle to the slaughterhouse. Each of them had his loves and duties, his life. Their names should not be forgotten.

In the year 1945 I would not have talked about all that. I would have considered it unnecessary and personal. Today, twenty-five years after the assassination, the situation is different. In this world not everything is in order by far. Therefore we must speak the truth—as we do in teaching—so that the young will know why we hate fascism so much.

The Heydrich period is not only a sad memory, it is something we have to learn from for the future.

There was no more resistance. Those few who were left burrowed deeper underground for the sake of survival, or joined the guerrillas in the mountains, where bands of them continued to harass the Germans in a small way throughout the occupation.

Sporadic, individual acts of sabotage (of the original "wooden shoe" variety) were sometimes performed. In eastern Moravia and Slovakia, occasional planes from England dropped arms and equipment; some trains were blown up, others were sidetracked, factory workers "slowed down" on the job.

Vlasta Chervinka, who managed to keep on feeding Eva in Theresienstadt for some time, was finally apprehended. The prison guard who had been helping him was caught smuggling food, and —under torture—revealed Vlasta's name. Vlasta was arrested and interrogated early in 1943. He was then imprisoned on the maximum security corridor of the Theresienstadt Small Fortress, near the cell where Paul Thummel was still in custody.

Paul Thummel (alias Franta, alias Dr. Steinberg) was now alias Peter Toman, a Dutch national, to preserve his anonymity. By the fall of 1943, Abendschoen, the Gestapo officer who had unmasked Thummel, had concluded his investigation and had prepared enough evidence for a trial. But the trial did not take place. Thummel's case was too embarrassing to Germans in high places to be exposed to the light of a court-martial, or even a civil court. As Peter Toman in maximum security he could do no harm to the German Reich. His case could wait.

On the Run

As the Allies began to penetrate Italy, our chances of eventual liberation from the prison camp increased, but so, also, did our chances of being immediately taken over by the Germans. The German armies were still in Italy, still strong in our area, and after Italy surrendered they were less inclined to leave the administration of anything, even prison camps, in Italian hands.

The Allies advanced very slowly in the beginning. After occupying Sicily, they crossed the Strait of Messina, then consolidated their bridgeheads on the mainland. We lay awake at night worrying. Would the Germans make a stand in our area? Or would they move to the north and make a line of defense there? This question was vital to the prisoners in our camp.

Jakubek and I were very much afraid that we would be sent north, to our deaths. With the Allies so tantalizingly close in the other direction, we decided to try once again to escape from the camp and to make our way across the front lines to the Allies. This would be very risky and needed careful preparation.

We started to accumulate a small hoard of bread and cheese to take with us, although we had to sacrifice our blankets in exchange for this food. We each acquired a sharp kitchen knife and the axe with which we used to work in the forest. One night we crept away, under the barbed wire, and ran south to the River Crati which flowed nearby.

Barefoot we went into the water and waded upstream so that our scent would be lost in case the prison guard dogs were used to track us. The water was ice cold. We waded upstream for about a mile on the stony river bed, during which time Jakubek's foot acquired a nasty cut. After that we swam across to the other bank and climbed up into the La Sila mountains.

The hardships of this trip were intensified by our fright and by the knowledge that we had left a secure bed and our friends in the barracks; but we knew that we were at least pointed toward freedom, and I had the feeling that we would make it.

All night we climbed the mountain, always trying to head as directly south as possible. Jakubek's foot became infected; he had started limping, but we went on until we became too hungry. In daylight we found a vineyard; the grapes were not quite ripe but we ate them to save our small store of food. We therefore got stomach aches and diarrhea.

The ground was rocky and the sun was hot, but the worst hazard was from the many kinds of planes which flew over us constantly. They shot at us, but we were not hit.

From time to time we saw a farmhouse, or people; but we made wide circles around such signs of life, to avoid being seen.

From the top of the mountain we could see the road that led north; we looked down and saw an unending stream of German troops and vehicles—tanks, cannons, troop carriers— all headed north. This gave us hope that the Germans were regrouping their defenses farther north and that we would not have to cross a fighting line.

Now, however, Jakubek's foot was becoming worse and worse. On the fourth day he decided that he could not go on. We sat down near a little spring and studied his injury.

His toe was quite black, and red stripes were running up his leg to his groin. Using my kitchen knife, I made a deep incision on the toe and all the blood and pus spurted out. I then tore up my dirty underwear, soaked it in the clear water, and bandaged the foot as well as I could.

We had no medicine or disinfectant, yet the next morning the stripes were gone. Jakubek was able to walk again, using only his heel; but we agreed to stay where we were for a while in order to rest.

From our eyrie we could see a farmhouse about three hundred yards downhill. We were weak from hunger and decided that the time had come when we must have some solid food. We decided to raid that farmhouse. In order to find out how many people we might have to cope with, we waited until mealtime when they would all return from the fields to eat.

When mealtime came we saw one old man, four women, and a host of children. When they were all indoors we left our perch, descended to the house, and boldly knocked on the door.

I stood with my axe poised in my right hand.

The old man opened the door. He looked as though he had stepped out of the Bible, with beautiful dark brown eyes and a white beard. I grabbed his shirt, pulled him toward me, and put the edge of my axe on his forehead.

"Give us bread, oil, eggs, and wine!" I said in Italian which I had learned in the Ferramonti-Tarsia prison camp.

He trembled all over. I lowered the axe but still held him with my left hand.

"We are all sons of Jesus Christ," he said and beckoned us in.

I was ashamed that I had used violence on this good man. When we stepped inside, the women were frightened by our appearance—we were unshaven, barefoot, shirtless, dressed only in ragged pants. But they fed us.

Jakubek sat at the table and ate—eggs swimming in oil, good bread and wine—while I stood guard. I noticed a double-barreled hunting rifle hanging on the wall.

"Is it yours?" I asked.

"Yes," he replied.

"It's not yours, it's mine now!" I told him. He gave me the rifle and a cartridge belt. Now we were armed with a gun.

Then I sat down to eat while Jakubek stood guard. I remember eating eight eggs swimming in oil, many pieces of delicious bread, and three or four glasses of good red wine. We felt fine after that meal.

The women of the house watched us eat their food voraciously and said, "Poor boys!" They washed and bandaged Jakubek's leg. The old man said, "I know that you are prisoners of war. I won't tell anybody that you came by. But, please, if you arrive at your destination, if you don't need that rifle any more, will you send it back to me? It is the only one I have."

We promised. We took his name and address. Then we thanked these good people for their kindness and left.

We continued our southward trek through the woods along the mountain top. Now I had a rifle slung over my shoulder and a cartridge belt around my waist. From time to time we shot a bird for food. Far down the hillside, on the road leading north, we could see the German armies still retreating. Planes flew overhead constantly.

On the eighth day of walking, we observed that the road was empty of vehicles. Also the air activity had almost stopped. We decided that we could now risk leaving the mountains and traveling along the road.

However, we decided to be cautious about it. We waited until nightfall, then descended and hid in the roadside ditch.

After a while we heard vehicles approaching and saw a line of the narrow slits of light which, for blackout purposes, were all that were permitted to escape of vehicular headlights. The tire noises did not sound like those of German vehicles; we held our breath.

Then we heard men's voices speaking English!

We had made it! We were saved! We were free! Silently we hugged each other in our ditch, overcome with joy.

We watched the platoons go by, and where there was a space between them I jumped onto the road and waved my arms, while the lamed

Jakubek waited. The cars stopped. I was blinded by a sharp light thrust in my face and ordered to "Drop that gun!"

I did so. "Put your hands up!" I did. A gun barrel pressed against my side, and I was taken to a jeep and questioned. "Who are you? Where are you from? How did you get here?"

Jakubek limped out and joined me. His appearance (unshaven, tattered, filthy, lean, infested with lice) reminded me that I looked just as bad and that the English had cause to be suspicious. After they determined that we were not Germans, they took us to a military field hospital where they shaved us, from head to toe, sprayed us, hosed us, and then fed us.

The next morning we were questioned at the Military Intelligence Headquarters of the British Eighth Army.

I was questioned by a pleasant, friendly British colonel, while a sergeant from the New Zealand Army took notes. The colonel asked me many questions about Prague—what school I had attended, where I had lived, my telephone number, and other seemingly trivial and unverifiable details. This seemed strange to me, until I learned, after I had passed muster, that the sergeant was a Czech émigré like myself, who verified everything I said.

Jakubek was also interviewed in this manner and also passed his test. They offered us a choice between joining our respective armies or going to England to work there.

Jakubek joined the Polish forces that were part of the British Eighth Army, fighting in Italy. I elected to go to England to join the Czechoslovak Air Force, which was part of the R.A.F. While waiting for the transportation which would take us to our destinations, we made up a package for the Italian farmer who had been so kind to us. In addition to returning his rifle, we sent him canned butter, bacon, coffee, cigarettes, and chocolates for the children. Then Jakubek and I parted, to go our separate ways.

In Britain, after completing my training, I became a navigator for the air force. I was assigned to Number 311 Czechoslovak Bomber Squadron.

Yalta and the Liberation

As the months passed, "Churchillky" brought news to the Czechs that the tide was turning against the Germans.

Even in the prisons the sparse grapevine put forth small tendrils of hope as the war dragged on.

In Theresienstadt, as in other prison camps, it became a matter of surviving until the Allies, and the liberation, arrived.

No one now expected the Germans to hold out for long; but as Allied pressure on the Nazis increased, so also did the Nazi pressure increase on the people under their domination. All prisoners expected daily to be shot before help arrived, so that no witnesses to German brutality would be left to testify.

At Yalta, Czechoslovakia had been assigned within the Russian sphere of influence. Therefore, although by April 1945 American armies had penetrated into western Bohemia as far as Pilsen, they did not move any closer. There they sat, eighty kilometers from Prague, because of the Yalta agreement.

The Czech Air Force (including 311 Bomber Squadron) strained like leashed dogs to go to the aid of their country, especially during the spontaneous, desperate Prague Uprising which took place at that time. Czech soldiers in London were eager to bomb the access roads to Prague, which were full of SS troops in heavy armor, moving toward the city. But the Czech Free Forces were not permitted to help their countrymen. Because of Yalta they sat too.

So the German reinforcements entered Prague, and the Germans attended to some last-minute business. Late in April an urgent order from the Prague Gestapo was dispatched to Commander Joeckel of the

Theresienstadt Prison. In accordance with this order, "Peter Toman, a Dutch national," was hurriedly shot. His death was duly recorded on page 11 of the Theresienstadt Small Fortress prison record: "Died April 20, 1945."

On May 9 the Russian armies entered Prague, defeated the Germans, and drove them out of Czechoslovakia.

The prisons were opened, the prisoners released. The Russians set up field hospitals to care for the pathetic remnants of humanity which poured out of them.

After the liberation, Czech traitors and collaborators were brought before Czech courts and confronted with their guilt. In addition to Curda, both K. H. Frank and Kurt Daluege were tried and executed.

Reinhard Heydrich. (Wide World Photos)

Karl Hermann Frank (Wide World Photos)

Vaclav Moravek

Professor Ladislav Vanek, alias Jindra

Jan Kubish (Czech Press Service)

Joseph Gabchik (Czech Press Service)

Major Adolf Opalka (Czech Press Service)

Heydrich's car after the assassination (Czech Press Service)

Gabchik's hat and raincoat, found at the place of the assassination. Also exhibited are the label sewn into Kubish's cap, Gabchik's bicycle, and the two men's briefcases. The posters ask, "Who knows the objects exhibited here?" (Czech Press Service)

Troopers standing guard at Heydrich's bier. The coffin is draped with an SS flag (Wide World Photos)

Heydrich's funeral procession from Prague Castle (Czech Press Service)

The wreckage and the murdered in Lidice (World Wide Photos)

The Karel Boromaeus Greek Orthodox Church on Ressl Street, Prague
(Czech Press Service)

The openings were originally the burial places of monks. The paratroopers put mattresses in them and slept there. (Czech Press Service)

Church Windows destroyed by machine guns fired from the opposite side of the street by the SS (Czech Press Service)

Identification of the dead Kubish in front of the church. Standing, in uniform, back to camera: K.H. Frank; third from right: Karel Curda; third from left: Dr. Otto Geschke, chief of the Gestapo in Prague (Czech Press Service)

The paratroopers tried to escape through the wall into the sewer system but did not succeed. (Czech Press Service)

Author Biography

While Jan Wiener was attached to Czechoslovak Number 311 Bomber Squadron in Wales, he flew twenty-four missions over Germany, France, and Holland as a navigator. Since he spoke fluent German, he was frequently asked to act as interpreter for General Josef Bartik, one of the leading officers of the Czechoslovak Intelligence in Great Britain and chief organizer of the plot to assassinate Reinhard Heydrich.

For a period of four months after the war, Wiener's squadron flew officials and their families from London to Prague. In September 1945, Mr. Wiener returned to Prague and found a position at the Language Institute teaching English. He remained at the institute from 1945 until 1948. By the time of the Communist coup d'etat in 1948 he was head of the English department, but he refused to join the Communist Party.

Consequently he was removed from his teaching position for involving himself in anti-state activities and for holding anti-peoples' attitudes. For more than three years he worked as a slag worker in the blast furnace at the Kladno steel mills near Prague. After Stalin's death in 1953, he was sent to work as a lumberjack in the Bohemian forests.

He was not allowed to return to the teaching profession until 1956, when he became an instructor in the language department of the Research Institute for Technical High Schools in Prague. The Czech government granted Mr. Wiener and his wife permission to visit the United States in 1965. He found a teaching position at the Windsor Mountain School in Lenox, Massachusetts, where for many years he taught modern European history and Sokol.

Author Chronology

1920: Jan G. Wiener was born in Hamburg, Germany where his father came from a Czech-German-Jewish family; the family returned to Prague with the rise of Hitler in 1933.

1939: Jan's mother, Franciska aided German-Jewish immigrants like Thomas Mann. She helped Mann and his family escape the Nazis but she was Terezin concentration camp where she subsequently died. Nineteen year old Jan followed his father to Yugoslavia where they hoped to get a visa to England and later the United States. Following the German occupation of Yugoslavia, Jan's father believed there was no way out. Exhausted and tired of running, he decided to commit suicide. This left Jan on his own while German soldiers were marching into Lubyana.

1940-1943: Jan made a daring escape in a cramped space under a train. However, he was caught and sent to a camp for political prisoners in Ferramonti Tarzia and another in Mongrassano Scallo, in Callabria, Italy. After numerous escapes and solitary confinements Jan reached a British platoon in the mountains.

1943-1944: Jan joined the Czech division of the RAF, the British Royal Air Force. Trained as a navigator, he served in the 311 Bomber Squad until the end of the war.

1945: After Jan's return to Prague in 1945 he began to study at Charles University and teach English at the Language School in Prague.

1948-1955: The Communists were now in power. Refusing to join the party Jan was arrested, and placed in a labor camp. He worked in a steel mill and as a forester in the Carpathian Mountains.

1955: Jan was now allowed to teach English at the Research Institute for Higher Education, History and Language Department in Prague.

1963-1965: After his second divorce, Jan fell in love with Zuzana Hloczek and they were married. Given permission by the Czech government Jan and Zuzana left Prague. They traveled to the United States where both of them became teachers at The Windsor Mountain School in Lenox, Massachusetts. The founders of the school, Max and Gertrud Bondy had founded the school in Germany, fled to Switzerland, then went to Windsor, Vermont. Sometime later they moved the boarding school to Lenox. Dr. Gertud Bondy, psychoanalyst at the school was one of the first women to study with Sigmund Freud in Vienna. She and her husband were parental figures as well as great educators. The school prospered from the 60s nearly to the end of the 70s. For a good while it was considered one of the most progressive schools in America.

1968-1975: After a year of teaching Jan was appointed head of the History Department at the Windsor Mountain School. So Jan and Zuzana decided to stay in the Berkshires of Massachusetts. This made for some political difficulties for Zuzana's family in Prague. But things were soon to get better. Jan's course, 20th Century Modern European History was partially the story of a man who had lived it himself. In addition to his academic work he also taught Sokol, a form of Czech gymnastics done with free weights. Beginning in 1968 and concluding in 1969 Jan wrote and published *The Assassination of*

Heydrich, which was brought out by Grossman/Viking. The book was highly praised by historian William L. Shirer in *The New York Times* and was later published in paperback by Fawcett Books.

1976-1980: Jan taught Modern European history at Williams College in Williamstown, Massachusetts and also at The Verde Valley School in Sedona, Arizona.

1980-1985: Jan taught at Schulle Schloss Salem, Baden, Wurttenberg, Germany.

1985-1989: Jan returned to the United States where he taught, lectured and worked at various other jobs.

1989: Back in Prague, Jan and Zuzana settled again, and this time he campaigned with Vaclav Havel before he was elected President of the Czech Republic.

1989-2010: Jan became a visiting professor of history at Charles University. He also assisted in the study abroad program of American University, Washington, DC, New York University Study Abroad Program and the Eces/Erasmus Program of Charles University. During this time Jan received the Medal of Merits of First Degree at Prague Castle's Vladislav Hall. The medal was personally presented by Vaclav Havel.

2010: Jan died peacefully at The Military Hospital of Prague. Although he was a war hero, his wish was not to have a military funeral. He called himself the wandering Jew and his ashes were spread according to his wishes in seven of the most beautiful places that he loved. These were, the Old Jewish Cemetery of Prague, among the ancient tombstones and family roots; at Masada in Israel; in the Atlantic Ocean by Provincetown on Cape Cod, an area Jan and Zuzana spent their vacations; in the Vitava River, which flows to the Elbe, and enters Hamburg where Jan was born; at a small graveyard in Stockbridge, Massachusetts where early American settlers and American natives are buried; on the grounds of Windsor Mountain School and at the lovely cemetery in Lenox, Massachusetts.

Compiled and written by Zuzana Wiener

Books by Jan Wiener

Always Against the Current by Jan Wiener, Konstanz University Press, 1994.
The Assassination of Heydrich by Jan Wiener, Viking Press, New York, 1969; Paperback edition, Pyramid Books/Fawcett, 1970.
The Assassination of Heydrich, paperback reprint, Irie Books, 2012.
Bojovnik: Vzdy proto proudu by Jan Wiener, Lidove Noviny Publishing, Prague, 2007.

Films about Jan Wiener

Four Pairs of Shoes: Czech TV documentary directed by Pavel Stringl, 1997.
Fighter: International documentary film directed by Emir Bar-Lev, 1998.
Two Homelands: Czech TV travel documentary, 1999.
Sky Above Europe: Czech TV documentary, Helena Trestikova, 2004.

Short Stories

Last Game, New York Times Sunday Magazine, 1991.

Military Decorations

Colonel of the Czech Air Force Retired
Czechoslovak War Cross
Czechoslovak Medal for Bravery in Action
British Defense Medal

Jan Wiener, My Friend

The world has lost a great fighter for freedom. I refer to Jan Wiener, my friend of 41 years who recently passed away at the age of 90 in Prague. As a member of the internationally revered Czech Bomber Squadron of Britain's Royal Air Force, Jan was the last of a line, the last, in fact, of a breed of heroes we will not see again.

Jan Wiener's narrow escape from the Nazis, and later, several prison camps in Italy is the stuff movies are made of. Not surprising that his life story was told in the award-winning documentary film, *Fighter*.

When I think of Jan and the years we shared as teachers at the Windsor Mountain School in Lenox, Massachusetts, I remember, most of all the phrases he used on a daily basis. To be sure I was listening, he would say "Meat?" And I would answer "Bones." This was the code that he used in a woodcutter's cabin in the mountains of Bohemia. He and his companion had stayed in a tiny cabin and after a long day of labor they would tell stories in the dark in their separate bunks. The word meat meant: "Are you awake?" Bones meant: "Yes, go on with your story!"

Meat and bones stories were exchanged by the two of us for many years. Once in *Night Flight*, a book I wrote about growing up in New Jersey, one of my characters, a man modeled after Jan, says, "Jews are not a religion, a name, a nation. They are like a long sometimes lonely river that runs to the great sea, the ocean of humankind. Do you understand what I mean?"

Jan told me that when he came to that part of the novel, he had watery eyes because he knew I was quoting something he'd said to me. "We are the same family, the same river." I described Jan's rugged good looks in another paragraph: "He wore the same old country mustache like the handlebars on a racing bike, the silver hair with the sun coming in through the open roof touching it and making it glisten like alpine snow." Speaking about that, he said, "I am not

Romany, like you." He also said, "I am an old fart, but I can still connect." By which he meant, with his fists. To the end, Jan was a brave and indomitable fighter. The size or force of the opposition was nothing to him.

Jan was 25 years older than his wife-to-be, the beautiful Zuzana, who was but 13 when they met, and who told her mother that same day, "He's my type." The widowed mother, Wilma, thought the same. He was her type too. But it was Zuzana, some years later, who married him. Wilma said to Jan: "It is all right now, while you are still young, but what will you do when you are old and she is young?" To that, Jan said, "I will get a younger wife." He didn't. There was no need, for Zuzana stayed young and lovely, now more than ever, after these many years.

Some people inspire in more ways than one. Jan was an inspiration to everyone who knew him. I knew many students at our school who wished not only to sound like Jan but despite their youth and his age, to look like him as well. I had a particular fondness for the way Jan spoke. His measured sentences, like the best prose, had the soft inflection of poetry.

Sometimes, over a glass of red wine, often Bikaver (blood of the bull in Hungarian), he'd recite the first paragraph of *A Farewell to Arms*. He spoke the one and two-syllable words, resonantly and methodically, so you could see the soldiers marching, feel the white dust of the roadbed rising and settling on the leaves of the trees and the coats of the soldiers. I think that by reciting that luminous paragraph, by doing it slowly and with quiet cadence, Jan taught me what it means to be a storyteller. And, saying that, I might add the word, *meat*, in case he is listening somewhere and would let the wind whisper, *bones*.

– Gerald Hausman

Lightning Source UK Ltd.
Milton Keynes UK
UKHW040037190822
407510UK00001B/13